Insomnia and Other
Poems, and Short Short Stories

by D.B. Pevney

Dedication

This book is dedicated to my dear friend Karen G. Strauss—my 'sunburst,' my inspiration, my muse. With love, for always.

David, Charlotte, North Carolina, June 28, 2025

Contents

Abuse the Muse

I thought my muse
     was selfless through,
Her inspiration
     my just due,

But never stopped I
     to consider
What ill my over-
     using did her.

I've run her ragged
     truth to tell,
Gone much too often
     to her well.

The Pierian Spring's
     about run dry,
I never asked the
     reason why.

But now I see
     what has befell,
I'm sure to end in
     writer's hell.

With damage done,
     what's left to say?
Perhaps that there
     will come a day

When ev'ry poet's
   cut down to size,
And all the muses
   unionize.

—DBP 10/1/23

All My Loves

There is love for our children
    and love for our pets
(And who knows that's maybe
as good as it gets)

And love for our parents
    and sibs and the rest,
And spousal love shouldn't
    be left unaddressed,

But then there are other
    varieties too,
And I ought to know 'cause
    I've gone through a few,

Well anyway next will come
    love for a friend,
It's a wonderful love and
    can last to the end,

And of course there's the
    hot love of partners for
    sex—
Perhaps that's my downfall,
    my prurient hex,

Then there are loves of old
    movies or books,

Or the foody-ish love of
    real talented cooks,

Some people love music,
    and some all the arts,
And some love sweet verse
    from poetical hearts,

Well, like I said, I've loved
    all these ways,
And maybe I'm done with
    a few nowadays,

But of all of the loves that
    there are, don't you see,
I love you the best way—
    that's romantically,

By which choice of term
    I just mean to say
The way that I love you's
    the 'in love with' way,

And in spite of your waffling
    and sometimes denial,
You also have loved me
    this way all the while.

—DBP 6/7/24

Ambiguity

My world is not orderly, but that isn't always a bad thing. Not always. I take comfort in ambiguity, in fluidity. Life should not be geometric shapes, hard borders, bright-line rules. Life should be fluid. Internally, societally, sexually.

Seldom does the imposition of order come without a terrible cost to the most helpless and most marginalized. Law should protect the weak, not subjugate them.

Labels rot the mind and poison the soul. We must be free.
Be, don't analyze. Feel, don't think.

I welcome the nameless, the classless. I gravitate to the edgeless flow, the swirls, the eddies, the spilling and mixing—I revel in these things and I hide in them. They protect me. Life's confusions caress. I do not fight them. Equanimity. Freedom of thought.

I look around: those who pay the most lip service to order, neatness, organization, classification often seem to have the most distressed psyches, the most turbulent souls.

—DBP 9/16/23

Anhedonia

In youth so many things delight
A sunny day, a starry night,

A favorite movie, show or book
From which hours of joy we took,

Also poems, songs, romance
An evening's flirting at a dance,

Perhaps even a dirty joke
In giggling whispers slyly spoke,

And most of all hot passion's
     throes,
Thrills of pleasure to our toes,

Such things come easy to
     the young
As from an endless well
     they'd sprung,

But it's a curiosity
That aging pleasures cease
     to be,

And growing old the joys
     we knew
Dwindle to a precious few,

Until at last it's manifest
That all we want is final rest.

—DBP 9/5/23

Anhedonia 2

They hide in darkness
in their rooms,
As antisocial weakness
dooms

Them to a life yet
living mourned,
With their own life
abandoned, scorned,

There is no joy, nor
mirth, no sun—
Their loneliness has
just begun,

The long years stretch,
but no tears cried,
So long ago the tears
have dried,

Now mere existence
day on day,
They stretch away all
dark and gray,

Days into months,
months into years,
No dawn nor daybreak
e'er appears,

The past is gone, they
     can't go back,
It all gets grayer,
     turns to black,

The only way time now
     can tend:
A lonely life, a lonely
     end.

—DBP 3/17/24

As Long as I'm Writing
I Haven't Lost

I try hard to become who
    I want to be,
And I know I'll become him,
    or he'll become me,

And dearly who I want to
    be I dare say,
Is one whose words blaze
    and in dark light the
    way,

I'm speaking of poets, the
    masters of verse,
And if I can be one, well
    then I could do worse,

Because poems are end-
    less, will never exhaust,
And as long as I'm writing
    one I haven't lost,

And while most are poorly,
    some will rise above,
And it's cliche I know but
    the best speak of love,

And I trust you can see
    that my heart leads my
    way,
As in rhymes I lament
    and in meters I pray,

So if writing of love is
    the answer to pain,
Then perhaps all this
    crazy is what keeps
    me sane.

—DBP 2/12/24

Asian Shrimp Dumpling

I like Asian, as do many:
Tempura, sushi, I'll take
any,

Rice and noodles, spicy
fish,
Sukiyaki—lovely dish!

But any dinner would
be skimpy
Without some dish a
little shrimpy,

And the shrimpiest of
all I trust
Are dumplings—and these
are a must,

Call 'em gyoza, shumai,
hakao,
They're all delicious anyhow,

And I can't help but to
wax winsome
When I start to speak
of dim sum,

And in closing I'll
be clear
That there is a
true wisdom here:

Whatever name you
give this treat,
The shrimp dumpling
is hard to beat.

—DBP 12/22/23 (at Red Bowl, our
local Chinese/Japanese/Asian
fusion place)

Avoid the Label

In this life we often
   see
Obsessive need for
   clarity,

And, sadly, because we
   are able
We give each varied
   thing a label,

And this all goes for
   people too,
A practice we should
   all eschew,

For every he or she
   or they
Should be allowed their
   separate say,

And not silenced by
   your own notions
Just to spare your own
   emotions,

Relationships likewise
   unspared,
For who of us is quite
   prepared,

To just let plain affection
    be
Not force it to
    conformity?

If someone's honest love
    you take
It doesn't them your "lover"
    make,

And it's OK upon
    reflection
To return a bit of
    that affection,

Society and your own
    mind
Will not be scandalized
    you'll find,

So that you will be
    better able,
In life and love: Avoid
    the label.

FREE. YOUR. MIND.

—DBP 9/22/23

Baked Men

Baked men
Waving club arms
They stand
In disordered rows
Lumpy and irregular
With eyes of clay
And feet which flake

—DBP 8/16/24

Be Brave to Be Honest

Going forward in this
    life
to friend or lover, man
    or wife,

Here's advice I have
    for you:
Be honest if you can't
    be true;

Just 'cause you have
    an open mind,
Others might not think
    in kind;

Prepare to give the
    reason why
If you are asked, and
    do not lie;

Don't try to put them
    on a spot,
But say your truth
    and worry not;

And if they feel that
    it's abuse,
You'll know it when
    they cut you loose;

But if they let the
    words go by,
And there's no falling
    of the sky,

Then understand, and
    count in it,
They still love, at least
    a bit.

—DBP 7/24/23

The Bear

I'd like to be a big old bear,
Big bears don't scare and
    they don't care,

Their feelings do not make
    them fret,
And leave them sad or much
    upset,

As winter comes they're
    busy at
Eating lots and getting fat,

Just busy getting food to
    cram in—
Hopefully a run of salmon,

And while they're proud,
    they never gloat,
About the thickness of
    their coat,

They don't make promises
    to keep,
They're unconcerned, just
    want to sleep,

And their long sleep is no
  big thing,
Just knowing that they'll
  wake in spring.

—DBP 1/6/24

The Bed-Bound Fart

It sometimes happens
    late at night,
The lights are off, you're
    tucked in tight,

When suddenly you have
    a start,
And realize you need to
    fart,

The blanket's warm, the
    bed is cozy,
You can't get up, you're
    far too dozy,

And though you are a
    lovely lass,
Even beauties must pass
    gas,

You agonize, the point is
    moot,
No compromise, you've
    got to poot,

And so you yield to the
    seduction,
Relief brought by rear-
    end eruction,

All will be well, so one
    assumes,
And you believe—
    until the fumes,

You need a plan, you've
    got to think,
But how can you with
    all that stink?

You only hoped and
    sought for peace
From sulphurous
    methane release,

But now it seems you're
    in despair,
As desperately you
    gasp for air,

To escape from this
    aroma,
You'd even risk a
    hematoma,

But you're never at
    a loss,
So up you jump, the
    blanket toss,

To stave off further
indignation,
An open window's
your salvation.

—DBP 1/17/24

Benefit of Bigamy

Marrying one
Can be kind of fun,

But marrying twice
They say is not nice,

Yet mouses won't do,
And mice, dear, are
    true,

And louse pairs so too
Are lice, dear, to
    you,

Well, now you should
    run,
'Cause her comes the
    pun:

Can one spouse
    suffice,
When you can have
    spice?

—DBP 6/27/25

Beshert

You and I were
   meant to be,
Words written before
Earth and sea,
And in Life's old
   and sacred tome,
It was ordained that
   we'd become
A match most even
   and enduring,
With strongest feel-
   ing, well ensuring
An endless tie bet-
   ween us two,
And whether to
   rejoice or rue,
Forever is the
   sacred bond,
Yea, unto death and
   then beyond.

—DBP 4/14/24

Best Laid Plans

The Bard observed that each
   and all
In life plays many parts;
As from each age to next
   we reach;
From endings to new
   starts.

When young we learn and
   go to school,
And then we in love sink;
Next spouse and babies
   are the rule,
With little time to think.

We then arrive in middle age,
   kids grown and spouse an 'ex'
With trembling hand we turn
   the page,
As doubts and fears perplex.

The way to go is not so
   clear;
The path leads into mist.
We plod ahead with growing
   fear,
And no one to assist.

We improvise another life,
    unsure what we've become.
And seek relief from stress and
    strife,
Exhaustion makes us numb.

But please do not from
    life withdraw,
With utterances scant,
Your artistry can overawe,
Your beauty can enchant.

For what's I say's no
    secret dear,
I'm pretty sure you
    know it,
For your new role in
    life is clear:
You are, my love, a
    poet.

—DBP 7/1/23

Best Selves

We pick and carp and
   criticize,
Find fault each in the
   other's eyes,

The years that passed
   well did their work,
Turned us into grump
   and jerk,

But I remember from
   before,
When I wasn't such a
   bore,

And you were happy,
   hopeful too,
Without so many things
   to rue,

Then I get happy and
   still see,
The best of you, and you
   see me.

—DBP 7/24/24

Birds of the Dawn

In the black just before
    dawn, the birds sing,
    eager.
Sunrise comes earlier
    now with each new
    day.
My heart sings also: new
    day, new month, new
    year—new everything.
The past had infinite
    branches, but all fused
    into one with each
    instant of time.
The future has infinitely
    more though, and they
    spread from horizon to
    horizon, an infinity, into
    a sunburst of mind, of
    thought, of reality—the
    possibilities are
    endless.
The birds are wise,
    they see, they know.
I have no wisdom but
    the wisdom of the
    birds, as they sing in the
    dark.

—DBP 1/1/23

Birds of the Day

The night is over.
We have reached
    the dawn—
The birds sing the
    sun up
And then take wing.
We set out on a new
    day.

—DBP March 2023

The Birth of
Sand

Ocean waves
Crash craggy shore
It seems with no effect.
Yet so on slave
For eons more,
Defying intellect.

—DBP 4/24/23

Bloomsday

A Saturday in June my
    dear, the year of '23,
The 10th it was by my
    recall (it's excellent,
    you see),

And to my lovely sewer
    room, in morning you
    came by
To make for me a magic
    day (I recall it with a
    sigh),

First 'Stop 20' to meet
    your beau, to eat
    and coffee sip,
Then onward to the
    UPS, a box of stuff
    to ship,

Then to that nice big
    library, for to peruse
    the shelves,
And there we had a
    grand old time, we
    sure enjoyed our-
    selves

Selecting books and
    taking them to
    comfy chairs to
    read,
I sat with you and
    wrote you poems,
    to satisfy my need!

We then went to the
    little park, and
    lounged beneath
    the tree,
Until so rudely were
    displaced by park
    security,

And there was too a
    diner lunch, and
    later still a roll
Of sushi at your
    favorite place
    (whose virtues I
    extoll)

And in between we
    sat abed and
    watched a movie
    rental
About Margaret's
    commune with

God ('twas rather
  sentimental)

My flannel shirt was
    old and ripped, a
    schmata's what you
    said
I was going to trash
    it, but I've kept it
    now instead,

Well anyway there's
    so much more I can
    recall and say,

But I'll close now and
    just remark it was
    a magic day.

—DBP 11/29/23

Book Bans

Isaac Asimov once
    said
Book-banners are all
    brain-dead,
And despite all their
    planning,
A book that's worth
    banning,
For sure is one worth
    being read.

—DBP 2/25/24

Book Love

How wonderful
That I cannot
Open a book
And read
Without
Thinking of
My love

—DBP at the exact
moment of the
winter solstice,
December 21, 2024,
4:25 AM

The Book Man

"What say you? Can you love the gentleman?
Read o'er the volume of the young man's face,
And find delight writ there with beauty's pen.
Examine every married lineament,
And see how one another lends content.
And, what obscured in this fair volume lies,
Find written in the margent of his eyes.
This precious book of love, this unbound lover,
To beautify him, only lacks a cover."

Shakespeare
Romeo and Juliet
Act 1, Scene 3
Lines 81-90

Books

Hardcover, paperback,
slipcased—inches thick
tomes, canvas or paper
dust-jacketed, magazines
and spiral-bound
pamphlets. On shelves, in
stacks, on furniture, in
boxes, by the bedside—
even in the bathroom.
Imagine the many hours,
days, months, years spent
in the most happy, happy
pursuit—black letters against
white, the feel of the paper,
the smell of new books
and the smell of old ones—
even the subtle sound of
a page being turned. No
fleshly pleasure can compare.
I have been blessed—God
smiled on me that long-ago
day when first I held a book!

—DBP 5/24/24

Books Always

I've never cared how it
    looks
That I hang out in
    library nooks,
Where I need to be—
That's where you'll
    find me,
Always surround-
    ed by books.

—DBP 5/14/24

Bunny Haiku

Sitting all alone
A pretty little bunny
Watches the sunrise.

—DBP 2/14/25

Bunny

The gloom can turn
    bright and it's funny
How a cloudy day fast
    can turn sunny—
I just think of you,
That's all I need do,
And it's all made OK
    by a bunny !

—DBP 8/18/24

Cafe con Amor

Our loves in this life
are so few,
But the one for good
coffee is true,
And while poetry's
nice,
Mere words can't
suffice,
I'll just ask you: One
sugar or two?

—DBP 2/28/25

Caligula's Court

Laws and norms are
   twisted, shattered,
Gone are all the things
   that mattered,

Decency and truth are
   dead,
Propaganda rules instead,

What's fake is real, and
   what's real fake,
So my eyes spin and my
   brains ache,

Brutality, injustice rule,
And everyone is that
   man's fool,

No rights left, and future
   grim,
These the gifts we get
   from him,

Life will be brutal, nasty,
   short,
Here in Caligula's court.

—DBP 1/22/25

Caryatid

A woman of marble, a
    thousand-yard stare,
such beauty, such grace,
    such a dignified air;

You stand with your
    sisters; you aren't alone,
performing your duties with
    siblings of stone;

Supporting the cornice,
    tympanum and frieze,
the triglyph, metope and
    such, if you please;

Been doing your job, and
    doing it well
over two thousand years
    (or so I've heard tell);

You're the picture of style;
    your look is iconic,
You vastly improve ev'ry
    feature Ionic;

The Parthenon stands in
    sun and in storm
thanks to your classical
    function and form;

For if any looter had taken
   the trouble
to move you, then we would
   have nothing but rubble.

—DBP 8/5/23

Catherine Morley
Rose (or, Rime of
the Ancient Mariner
Meets Edgar Allan
Poe)

It was a dark and stormy night
    and in the tavern there I sat
Amid a dour assemblage—none
    given o'er to cards or chat.

The burning fire in the grate
    did little to dispel the gloom.
The wind then howled and
    thunder flashed—the door
    banged open with a boom.

A tall man came into the bar, chill
    and dripping from the storm,
He called a pint and neared the
    fire, and stood a moment to get
    warm.

And in his face we saw a look of
    sadness and dismay as well,
He saw our gaze, a swallow took,
    made up his mind his tale to tell:

"Friends I see you mean no harm,
    and likewise I wish none to you,
I tell you now a tale so strange,
    I doubt that you'll believe it's true.

"But true it is, so give an ear, and
    list to what I have to say
Of ominous events that passed—
    they happened on this very day.

"I'd written with a lady friend,
    quite close by this vicinity
A woman of some standing here—
    so went the story she told me.

"After quite a long exchange, but
    never meeting face to face,
It was decided I'd come here, and
    meet at her ancestral place.

"The train I took arrived with speed,
    I set about to find a brougham,
But nary was a one for hire to take
    me to the lady's home,

"For each time I would then refer
    to whom it was I'd come to meet,
The cabby suddenly would pale,
    refuse to me a carriage seat.

"I walked the miles bag in hand,
    and found the house in afternoon,
I met the lady—she was fair, as
    pretty as a rose in June.

"Her voice was of the sweetest
    tone, and talking with her did
    delight,
Her grace and manner worked to
    charm—I never saw a nicer sight.

"And she prepared a picnic lunch,
    and 'neath a tree we sat and
    talked,
The sun was warm, the birds all
    sang, and I was tired from all I'd
    walked,

"I fell asleep and slept the day
    and dreamed of lovely company—
At sunset I woke with a start, no lady
    sitting next to me.

"The air was chill, the birds were
    gone—I looked about and saw
    no tree,
I was alone, the lady gone, all
    dismal was what I could see,

"For I was in a weedy field of
    stones for those who ever
    sleep,
And on the closest stone to me,
    the name of her I'd come to
    see, carved in letters deep.

"I've walked the evening long and
    wet, I lost my bag along the way,
Finally found myself here, and that
    is all I have to say."

He sat in silence then but I
    a question fairly had to pose:
"What was the lady's name," I said.
    He answered "Catherine Morley
    Rose."

Then I stood and shook my head,
    and paced the wooden floor,
"That lady gave you lunch today—
    dead twenty years or more."

I never saw the man again, but often
    late at night,
I think upon the tale he told, it
    gives me quite a fright.

I shiver as in bed I lay, and as
    my eyes I close,

I think about that eerie day, and
Catherine Morley Rose.

—DBP 2/19/24

Caution to the Activist Poet (or, With Great Power Comes Great Responsibility)

Poetry's more than fancy
    flight,
Coffee-powered in the
    night;
It can be truth made
    literate
To expose the hateful
    hypocrite;
For 'us' aspiring to be
    'we,'
It promotes internal
    honesty;
And poetry helps us to
    detect
Shortcomings in the
    intellect;
But careful when exposing
    lies:
Let's not miss what's before
    our eyes;
The elegance that we
    enthuse,
Makes it easy to
    abuse;

Because we are the
    instigators,
Beware lest we become
    the haters.

—DBP 7/14/23 (Bastille Day)

The Charms of
Book Collecting

Some volumes
    sleep in decades'
    dust,
Redolent in wordy
    must,

Others fresh from
    modern presses,
Lure us in with
    inked caresses,

Gilt-edge pages
    leather-bound,
Rustling make a
    magic sound,

Shadows in a quiet
    room,
Lamplight cheerful
    piercing gloom,

As many books as
    we are able,
We stack here at our
    oaken table,

To read away the
    welcome dark,
As solemn chimes
    the hours mark,

We drift along to
    shores that seem
To come to us as
    in a dream,

Wander groves of
    knowledge vast,
Ideas enough a
    life to last,

Measured verse our
    pains to ease,
And volumes of
    philosophies,

Historically set
    depictions,
Or purely novel-
    istic fictions,

Enabled other
    lives to live,
We feel the power
    words can give,

So in a life with
    pleasures few,
I recommend the
    books to you,

I'll starve to save
    up my last penny
To buy, 'cause you
    can't have too
    many.

—DBP 11/20/23

The Circles

Shadowy circles, grim associations,
The last happiness far off now, irrevocable.
Slowly spreading, circle to circle,
The old long gone, the rest old now.
We wither and die, dead before our deaths.
And so it spreads, never ceasing, never slowing.
It will reach beyond us:
There is no refuge.
The circles have no color now, only gray and black.

—DBP 12/3/22

Coffee Aspirations

Shambling to the kitchen
   plod,
Fumbling dazed you grab
   a pod,

Pry open then the K-
   machine,
Try to find a mug that's
   clean,

Insert the pod into
   the slot,
Don't worry you don't
   need a pot,

Follow steps the
   way you oughtta,
Make sure to put in
   enough water,*

Hit the button, hear
   the stream,
The hiss of that de-
   lightful steam,

Soon the heavenly
   aroma
Starts to lift you from
   your coma,

It fills the cup with
      happy black,
Though cream or
      sugar you may lack,

Add whatever suits
      your taste
And blow on it in
      eager haste,

Take a sip and feel
      the rise,
Sleep now banished
      from your eyes,

Oh glorious caffeine
      for you—
Praise the God who
      gives our brew!

(*ouch!)

—DBP 12/5/23

Coffee

Among the greatest
　　sights I've seen:
A deepish cup of
　　brew serene,
To spark the wisdom
　　of a sage,
Or else a mug of
　　creamy beige,
To even out the
　　furrowed brow
And lighten up the
　　soul somehow.
Light or sweet or
　　bitter black,
On its own or with
　　a snack,
Morning, afternoon
　　or night,
Whatever time, the
　　hour's right.
Well-iced is the summer
　　way,
Or steaming on a
　　winter day—
I'd even trade in my
　　diploma
To smell that magical
　　aroma!

No matter where in
   life I go,
I'll always have my
   cuppa joe.
I 💜 Coffee

—DBP 3/6/24

Crickets

I'm restless,
I'm thoughtful,
I'm pre-occupied,
I'm amorous,
I'm horny.
I'm filled with
Love and lust, and
Ideas. My mind, my
Heart, my soul, are
Dragged on journeys
I know not where:
I always find out
When I get there.
I need no drugs.
My mind is a sack of
Crickets, all struggling
To get out at the same
Time, but controlled,
Somehow controlled,
Lord knows how
Controlled.
Somehow focused.
Focused.
The crickets are able
To focus.
Way to go, crickets!

—DBP 3/24/23

David and Karen
(Sitting In a Tree)

David and Karen,
Sitting in a tree
K-I-S-S-
I-N-G.
Maybe love,
And might be lust,
But David's poems
Are a bust.

—DBP 6/21/25

The Dead

The dead do come to
   us in dreams,
But not at our behest
   it seems,

They're unexpected,
   come unbidden,
From their world far-
   off and hidden,

And never in the light
   of day,
But in the shadows
   have their say,

They don't give counsel
   to inspire,
But only say what they
   desire,

The ones we love we
   wish to stay,
But break of dawn
   they fly away,

And if we try to hold
   them then,
They're gone, and never
   seen again.

—DBP 6/18/24

Death Dreams

When I sleep I sometimes
    dream
Of how the place to come
    might seem,

Which leads me on to
    wonder then,
Do departed dream again?

Do they sleep within their
    sleep?
And deathly dreamy counsel
    keep?

And in the gloom and dark-
    ness there,
Remember times of light
    and air?

Do they miss their earthly
    days,
Forever lost in obscure
    haze?

Or with minds emptied
    simply doze?
It's sad that no one living
    knows.

—DBP 6/21/25

Death of a Book Lover

All my life I've had
    the need,
The powerful desire
    to read,

Each library and
    quaint bookstore
Has always left me
    wanting more,

I'd always give them
    second looks
For leading to my true
    love: books,

Perhaps books never
    made me wise,
And just put mileage
    on my eyes,

While helping me escape
    from strife
They limited my
    social life,

But any ill they've done
    to me,
Was worth the trouble,
    don't you see?

Whether comical or
    tragic,
The worlds they take
    me to are magic,

My mind is never
    overwrought,
But just delights in
    each new thought,

And ev'ry notion I
    suppose
Conveyed to me by
    poem and prose

Has left me with a
    sense of wonder,
A spell I'm happy to
    be under,

And though each
    paragraph and page
Has brought me closer
    to old age,

And knowledge that
    the end is near,
I will not cringe, nor will
    I fear,

When death arrives
    I will not grovel,
But grab with my last
    strength a novel,

And when I'm just a
    lifeless shell,
There is one thing
    would serve me well,

Your help can surely
    death's blow soften:
Please toss that book
    into my coffin.

—DBP 8/1/23

The Death of Pure Love, a Fable after Aesop

A ram and a goat and a ewe all lived in the same meadow. Both the ram and the goat courted the ewe. The goat was ugly, he had no art, was carried away by no passion, and lacked imagination. But his love for the ewe was pure and true. The ram was fiery, tempestuous, very randy, given to flights of fancy and badly-behaved. His love for the ewe was, if not entirely pure, also true. She loved the ram, but she feared him for his passion, for his unpredictability and his wayward ways.

The ewe distanced herself from the ram and took the steadfast goat for her mate. The ram, dejected, left the meadow and stayed far away.

One night a pack of hungry wolves descended on the meadow. They found the goat and the ewe. The goat did his best to defend the ewe, but had limited weapons and a decided lack of viciousness. He fought but succumbed to the violent onslaught; both goat and ewe were devoured until only bones remained. The wolves then sought out the ram, and finally located him in his self-imposed exile. The ram pawed the earth; faced with death, he responded in kind. He gave way to bloodlust and fought not to defend himself, but to inflict pain on his enemies and make them bleed and die. While horribly wounded himself, he battered and gored and slaughtered every last wolf.

Thereafter, he hobbled back to the meadow on shaky legs, leaving a trail of blood behind him. He looked upon the bones of his beloved and wept before he died, because he knew that if she had chosen him she would still live. His grief at her pointless death overwhelmed him as he closed his eyes for the last time.

Moral: Pure love is a fine dish, but romance, passion, imagination and lust are great condiments.

—DBP 2/4/23

Devils

The devils-in-chief are
    both clueless and cruel,
And it's hard to tell which
    is the stupider fool,

They smile and look at
    you right in the eye,
And every word spoken
    is just a damn lie,

They explain why it's good
    just to trash everything,
Heedless of death and
    destruction they bring,

They have so much wealth
    but they really can't spare
Any funds for the poor
    'cause they really don't
    care,

It's good for the nation to
    increase their wealth,
And now they're in solid,
    they've no need of stealth,

And every billionaire that
    you can see

Must gain extra wealth
    grinding down you and
    me,

The rich need more tax
    breaks, so just you be-
    ware,
The poor and the old will
    lose medical care,

They need a new yacht
    and another jet plane,
Who cares if kids die?
    It's all so insane,

The environment now is
    a burning cess-pit,
They'll protect all their own
    from all of the shit,

And of course it's important
    to screw our allies,
Just sell 'em out quick and
    then spit in their eyes,

If there's any justice these
    devils may know,
If they don't find it here,
    they will far below,

Fried up by some demons
    in sizzling oil,
In torment they'll shriek
    as they burn and they
    boil,

They'll pray for an end-
    ing for all of their pain,
But having died once,
    they can't die again,

No choice now but suffer
    for every last crime
Forever—and that is a
    very long time. ☺

—DBP 2/23/25

Diarrhea

Intestines churning,
Asshole burning,
I sit me down to
    squirt,

And toilet pound
With splatty sound
No way I can avert,

This fateful dump
My guts will pump
Forever now I think,

As with a groan
I sit alone,
Surrounded by the
    stink.

—DBP 5/5/24

Dirty Doggerel, or
Talent for Trash

In contemplating subjects
   few are fonder,
And rarely do they cause
   my thoughts to wander
Like the one to me that
   is a spell or hex,
And that dear lady is
   the realm of sex.

It isn't that I'm altogether
   randy,
Or the rhyming that springs
   up is always dandy,
And never would I injure
   or abuse
My reader with the verse
   that I enthuse.

But carnal rumination
   captivates,
And the muse that brings it
   rarely hesitates,
The words pour forth, my
   heart is all a-flutter:
Alas, my "happy place" is in
   the gutter!

—DBP 6/27/23

Do Not Forget

Think of me;
Remember me.
The same sun shines
    on me as on you;
Know that every time
    you feel it's warmth.
My feet tread the
    same earth as yours;
Know that every time
    you take a step.
I breathe the same air;
Know that every time
    you inhale.
The same God smiles
    down on me as on you;
Know that every time you
    think of your place in the
    Universe.
I will always be here;
Know that.
Do not forget.

—DBP 9/19/23

Dog Bath

The topic on which
  I now speak
Is what to do when
  doggies reek,

Into the bathtub
  they must go
Without much fuss
  or much ado,

Get some water in
  the tub,
A pitcher and the
  will to scrub,

A goodly dab of
  kids' shampoo
And lots of towels
  work for you,

Soapy suds are
  really neat,
Scrub back, belly
  and the feet,

And if the heinie
  you forget,
Later on you will
  regret,

When you're done
    there's little more;
So there's a river
    in the floor?

It doesn't matter,
    don't ask why,
Be sure to get the
    doggie dry,

And that's it then,
    that's how you do it,
And so you see there's
    nothing to it.

—DBP 11/28/23

Don Quixote

I live adventures that I
    find,
Tilt at windmills in my
    mind,

Sometimes I win, more
    often lose,
And get knocked flat,
    and bleed and bruise,

I rise and shake the dirt
    off me,
And climb the next hill
    that I see,

So why the squire?
    Where's the need?
More noble is the
    solo deed!

But my heroics must
    be sung,
For thus are heroes
    ever young,

To spread my exploits
    would be hard
Without a true and
    trusty bard,

And so we travel far
and wide,
Me and Sancho by
my side,

Let my fame travel
as it must,
Even when I lie in
dust.

—DBP 1/28/24

The Drag Brunch

I had bought tickets to the drag brunch the previous week. This was at the end of a hot July, but the theme was to be very Halloween—the show was entitled "Witchy Woman."

I prepared by going to the bank and taking out $100 in the form of twenty $5 bills. I gave little thought to the theme, even forgetting to mention it to the date I asked, my cross-dressing friend Holli.

Saturday rolled around. I picked up Holli at her trailer park. She was dressed in pink, as Barbie. Of course then I remembered that the theme was not Barbie and told her. Nevertheless, she was happy to go as Barbie. Just as well. I was in cutoff jean shorts, sandals and an "I Read Banned Books" T -shirt.

I made the trip into Uptown, to the artists' coffee house venue. We were seated at the bar by a pleasant mustachioed young man dressed in a black 'Wicked Witch of the West' costume—high black peaked hat and all. Margaret Hamilton would have been proud.

By swiveling my stool, I found that the spot commanded a view of the entire floor and all of the surrounding tables and spectators.

The show began, with the 'mistress of ceremonies' cracking the obligatory joke that "it costs a lot to look this cheap" along with the usual jesting promises of post-show back room sex for a sufficiently large 'contribution'

The semi-intimate setting was perfect: no stage, with the dancing and lip-synching queens circulating to grab the $5s and $10s enthusiastically waved at them.

The costumes were elaborate and authentic, the music fun and loud, the atmosphere raucous, and the queens sexy and congenial—more than happy to pause on their rounds and pose for a quick selfie.

It was a great show—two hours went by as quickly as it took me to go through nineteen of my twenty $5 bills.

Afterwards, I got a photo op with 'Elvira, Mistress of the Dark.' She was big-breasted, black beehive-wigged and beautiful, looking for all the world like the real Cassandra Peterson in makeup and costume. I was enchanted, almost overcome with a feeling of childlike wonder curiously mixed with incipient lust.

The all-too-brief moment ended. Some of the queens had already made their way to a poorly concealed back room they had been using as a changing area—no door, and right next to the unisex bathroom, guaranteeing a steady stream of passing foot traffic and consequently a more or less complete lack of privacy.

Costumes and accessories were coming off—a very large queen was minus her wig and a good deal of her makeup, and she was now a chubby and entirely bald man.

Part of me wanted to stay, to see what my crush 'Elvira' looked like in her more everyday state.

I remembered the words that Holli used to repeat frequently when we first met: "it's all about maintaining the illusion."

She was right, of course. I spun on my heel, collected her, and walked out into the summer afternoon, hot-asphalt-smelling parking lot, squinting in the bright sunshine—my illusion behind me, safe in the recent past, in the comfortingly-shadowed cafe.

—DBP 7/29/23

Dream-Life

In dreams sometimes
    they come to me,
And then the dead
    once more I see,

They seem to live again
    and walk,
And just as when alive
    they talk,

And what seems so
    much stranger still,
Is while the dead do
    what they will,

The living are not there
    instead,
In the dream they are
    the dead,

And in the dream I think
    I'm lost,
Or perhaps that I
    have crossed,

That I have died, some-
    how forgot,
But something in me
    knows that's not

The truth about what's
    going on,
That I'm just dreaming
    and not gone,

And when I'm almost sure
    that's right,
The dead, now silent,
    leave my sight,

My waking up will then
    confuse,
As I try my wits to use,

Remember who's alive,
    who's dead,
It takes a minute for
    my head,

To get it straight, then
    I'm OK,
Ready for the coming
    day,

For I can now rest
    well assured
That this delusion
    has been cured,

The living yet have life
and breath,
The dead as safely
rest in death.

—DBP 11/30/24

Dreams

I'm happiest, it seems
Adrift on slumber's streams,
My thoughts are of you,
And you're asleep too—
We dream us in our

    dreams

—DBP 1/7/25

Dreams of Flight

There was a hatchling, a fledgling,
She perched, trembling, day after day
At the edge of the nest.
She dreamed of flying.
One day, she gathered her courage,
And jumped. Out into space…and
Down…then surprise and relief and
Elation and up!
Toward the sky, toward the clouds,
Toward the sun.
And so again day after day, through
The summer, through a lifetime.
The bird became old, the world
Became cold, the sky became wind
And rain and storms.
The bird was pelted, beaten,
Exhausted, grounded.
She lay in a puddle,
Freezing, wings broken.
Her eyes closed,
She dreamed of flying.

—DBP 1/20/23

Ellen's Cold—a Celebration of Excess Verbiage

Ellen sat at the little table in her little kitchen, shoulders slumped and head hung over her hot cup of coffee. She eagerly inhaled the steam—in between coughs.

That she had overslept—after trying to get to sleep for most of the night—and that she would be late for work should she go—were facts, beyond dispute.
Whether she should be going in at all was an open question.

Ellen grabbed a tissue and quickly caught the stream of watery mucus that had started from her nose, before it could drip into her cup. She thought about that and the notion nauseated her—if it happened she would have to dump the coffee, ditch the mug and start the coffee-making process all over.

She mulled on it further, and decided that she was fixating on a bizarre notion—further proof of the effects of her illness.

Over the next several minutes, and with a good deal of blowing-coughing, she finished her cup, while trying to think of nothing at all—at which exercise she failed miserably. Instead of thinking of nothing, her mind raced.
She thought of a hundred things in quick, disorganized succession. The headache that had slowly been coming on now erupted in full vigor, caffeine notwithstanding.

Ellen decided to call in sick and go back to bed.

But first she needed to go to the bathroom.

She stood and shivered an urgent I-really-need-to-pee shiver, hugging herself in her big white terrycloth bathrobe. She then began to make her way to the bathroom, her oversized fluffy lavender slippers making a rapid 'shoop-shoop' noise as she walked. Arriving at the toilet, she pulled up the hem of the robe and gathered the soft bulky material to one side, then awkwardly stooped to pull her panties down around her ankles with her other hand—nearly losing her balance in the process. She shivered again, pulled up the lid, and sat on the freezing toilet seat.

Up until that point she had managed to restrain her bladder, but contact with the cold seat triggered an involuntary gush. The stream was forceful and voluminous, the pressure-hose sound amplified by the porcelain resonating chamber. Ellen took a momentary satisfaction in that. "Well, at least my plumbing still works," she mumbled audibly to herself.

As her urgency—and her urination—began to subside, Ellen's mind began to dart about again. This time she tried to direct it to the mental list of things that she had originally wanted to get done today. However, whatever cognitive order she was able to impose quickly began to evaporate, and she abandoned her attempt at organized thought in anxious disgust. She wiped, stood up with an effort, and gave her hands a quick rinse in water that was much too cold and would take much too long to run hot.

Hands dripping, and with renewed shivering, Ellen commenced shuffling again, this time back to the bedroom. She shucked the robe, dumping it on the floor, and collapsed into the now-cold bed, pulling up the comforter all the way to her now-freely-running nose. She was going to have to wash the bedding anyway.

The shades were still pulled down, but she could see the day brightening outside.

She still needed to make her phone call.

—DBP 12/5/23

Version Two

Ellen was sick. She had a cold. She had a cup of coffee and decided to call in sick to work. She peed and went back to bed.

—DBP 6/28/24

Epitaph

All my life underachieved,
Chances lost can't be
    retrieved;

Did fortune come? It came
    and went;
Can't say where the cash
    was spent;

And if not fortune, what of
    fame?
No, I have no famous
    name;

Well, at least I had a kid?
No, not true, I never did;

For while I lived both fast
    and loose,
I never got to reproduce;

I've left no mark, done no
    deed great,
And in the end, I just don't
    rate;

No legacy for the
    misbegotten,

So soon I'm gone, I'll be
    forgotten.

"Non Fui
 Fui
 Non Sum
 Non Curo"*

—DBP 7/19/23

(*"I was not
    I was
    I am not
    I care not"
Epitaph often seen on ancient
Roman tombstones along the
Appian Way)

Erato*

I see her as an
    angel, robed in
    shim'ring light
Her voice is music
    to the ear, her face
    enchants the sight;

Above all else, her
    words are sweet,
    and pleasingly evoke
The thoughts and
    feelings we may have
    which our words never
    spoke;

She sings the beauties
    and the loves she's
    seen through history,
And doesn't question but
    accepts the ageless
    mystery;

And even while rejoicing
    in each love thus well
    requited,
So comforts she the
    lonely too, the
    wretched and
    benighted;

While happy hearts
    she lifts on high
    when in love they
    fall,
She also speaks to
    downcast hearts who
    rise up to her call;

And so at last when our
    words fail and we've
    no more to say,
Her lines of verse show
    us the path, make
    easier our way.**

(*Erato is the muse of lyric—as opposed
to epic—poetry, and especially of love
poetry.)

(**In Latin, 'poetry' and 'consolation'
were synonymous; the word 'consolatio'
was used for both.)

—DBP 9/28/23

Escape from Superjail

For offending I was
    blocked,
And in the doghouse
    I was locked,

More sturdy-built than
    any jail,
So grim and fearsome
    each detail:

The bars of adamantine
    steel
Would make the bravest
    hopeless feel,

The walls of stone some
    three feet thick
Cannot be breached by
    force or trick,

The doors are iron, rusty
    black,
Once locked there is no
    going back,

The lock so massive and
    so strong,
You'd try, keep failing all
    day long;

Bust out? Nobody has
  a prayer,
There just is no way
  outta there!

Escape? No chance! No
  how! No way!
Once you're in, you're
  there to stay!

Beyond the power of
  a genie,
David Blaine or H.
  Houdini;

Except for someone
  REALLY good—
He's the only one
  who could;

You wonder who? Don't
  waste your time—
He's the guy who
  wrote this rhyme.

—DBP 4/28/24

Eternity, But Less a Year

My love won't last for-
    ever, dear,
Eternity, but less a
    year;

You know I speak no
    empty words
In verse of flowers,
    suns and birds;

And if you ever have
    a doubt,
Here's something you
    should think about:

With honest love, not
    phony tears
I came back after
    thirty years;

But then some more
    won't hurt I guess,
What's several decades
    more or less?

I'll never stop, though
    it may hurt,
Until they dump me
    in the dirt;

And while it's true you
won't have me,
At least you'll get my
poetry.

—DBP 5/20/24

Evangeline 2
(with Apologies
to Longfellow)

I wait for you the live-
long day,
So go my years and life
that way,

I pine and search, know
what I mean?
It's something like
Evangeline,

Near misses all down
through the years,
Not sure of you but I've
had tears,

And when days dwindle
down to few,
You'll find me and I'll
find you,

I do not ask or wonder
why,
We'll find each other—
then one will die.

—DBP 1/9/24

Excrucior

My soul won't calm, nor
    ardor cool,
My scattered thoughts
    can know no rule,

My heart beats thunder,
    eyes flash lightening,
And spirit writhes in fire
    frightening,

My thoughts and mad-
    ness flail away,
But yet survive another
    day,

And each sunrise con-
    sume and burn,
And each sunset a new
    death earn.

—DBP 7/12/24

Fall

In 🍂 fall the pretty colors
   come up
Even though they push
   back ⚪ sunup,

It's also true the 😟 temp
   does drop
But that just makes me
   feel on top,

I think more clear, less
   like a fool
When the air is crisp
   and cool,

But I can still be some-
   what silly,
When breezes blow
   and it gets 😬 chilly,

October brings a
   cheerful scene
With costumed ghouls
   on 👻 Halloween,

And at the risk of
   feeling jerky,

I AM a fool for   pie
       and   turkey,

And with any luck,
       you know,
By New Year's Day we
       will have   snow,

And really I'm not down
       at all—
I don't know why they
       call it fall.

—DBP 9/20/24

Fall 2

Ancient trees, old moss covered, thickly-vined, branches interweaving, mostly bare and skeletal, brown leaves strewn and rotting in cold damp.

A forest dark, no cheer, only nightbirds and bats.

What was a clearing, the ruins of a long-abandoned abbey, ivy-overrun, tendrils clinging, walls knocked down by stone-strewing years.

The overgrown field beyond strangely studded with weathered headstones, placed seemingly at random, cracked, half buried, many askew, some thrown down by time. Souls long dead.

No springs, no summers, cold rain and sparse snows only, no roaring fireplace to cheer, always October or November.

—DBP 7/9/23

Falling Off a Log*

Through miles of verses
    I jog,
You might think it seems
    quite a slog,
But me loving you,
Writing poetry too,
Is like falling off that
    old log.

—DBP 1/21/25

*Seriously, it's easier
to write the poetry
(as bad as it is), than
to NOT write it.

Farts

A subject very near
    my heart
Is the oft recurring
    fart,

Some are pffts and
    some are BRAAAPs
And some make wet
    and messy craps,

Some are silent, deadly
    too,
Get too close and you
    will rue,

Pretty girls with cutesy
    toots
Will singe your hair
    down to the roots,

Truck drivers at a
    greasy spoon
Will make you want
    to die real soon,

The pooch is often
    man's best friend,
But stay away from
    their rear end!

When passing gas
    you must beware,
Please be cautious—
    have a care:

You think a puff is
    all you'll get,
Alas, oh no, you feel
    it's wet!

You shat your pants,
    no, it's not fair—
To Walmart for some
    underwear!

—DBP 3/16/24

Feline Thoughts

What kitties likely
    contemplate
Is a matter of debate,

Perhaps they think of
    hunting birds
With furry thoughts
    that have no words,

Or maybe something
    just as nice:
To ambush unsuspecting
    mice,

Then taking leave of
    such attacks,
Their minds wander to
    favorite snacks,

Whatever is their dearest
    wish,
A dish of cream or scrap
    of fish,

Toms think ladies,
    ladies toms,
Kittens dream about
    their moms,

On sunny days they
think of rain,
And when it rains, of
sun again.

—DBP 6/12/25

Final Voyage?

I think of how confused I am,
Puzzle why you bless then damn,

And you well know my turning mind,
Won't rest until I jot some kind

Of poetistic imagery
(If overblown, we'll, that's just me),

My ranging thoughts bring forth the
    sight
Of you, the brilliant orb of light,

While 'neath your sunburst on the sea
The ship that races on is me,

I seem to fly with sails unfurled
That billow candor to world,

And in so doing play the Bard
To verse to all true love dies hard,

And as each day in sunset ends
The same is true of dearest friends,

The wind has calmed, the sailing's
    done,
The ship bereft now ends its run,

The sun's last ray's a final breath,
The night that comes is black as
    Death,

But even after death it's said
Some ghost ships rise up from the
    dead.

—DBP 9/16/23

Five-Four-Three

If I were a dog,
I'd jump on you,
Wag my tail.

If I were a cat,
I would bring you
My dead bird.

—DBP 5/9/23

Fools and Lawyers

The lawyer is a motley
    fool,
A clown and poser as
    a rule,

Who struts and capers
    all along
And loves to sing a
    silly song.

And when he gets
    before a jury,
He is full of sound
    and fury,

But as with Shake-
    speare's comic
    actor,
Reality's no major
    factor,

And hardly ever truth
    is sought,
So all his efforts come
    to nought.

—DBP 3/4/24

Garden of Love*

I found the Garden of Love
Where morn came ev'ry hour,
And Helios above
Shone down in ev'ry flower;

Thoughtful I went home,
The nights were long and dark,
And e'er my thoughts would roam
To that joyful sunny park;

So I went back to the same,
To see how blossoms fared,
Was sorry that I came,
Then angry, then just scared:

The flower beds were gone,
With nary one to save,
I saw by light of dawn
Each had become a grave.

—DBP 2/3/24

*apologies to William Blake

Gerbil

The gerbil is a strange
    animal.
It doesn't exist in nature,
    only in pet stores.
Where did it live before
    there were pet stores?
How did it evolve?
The gerbil only eats
    packaged pellets
    and lettuce from the
    store.
So if a gerbil escaped
    it would have to hide
    out in a dumpster
    behind a store, hoping
    for some lettuce, which
    would probably be
    rotten anyway.
Or else the poor thing
    would die.
I wonder if they find a
    lot of gerbil skeletons
    in and around dumpsters?

Poor gerbil!

—DBP 5/3/24

Geriatric Love

Sometimes I glimpse
    a distant view,
    I hesitate to say;
In this idyll I'll live
    with you in some far
    future day.

I see it through a
    fog of time
    still many years
    ahead,
When we are both
    long past our prime
    (but before when we are
    dead).

We'll be together then
    my sweet, but when is
    hard to say;
I'll try to sweep you off
    your feet (tough on
    the vertebrae).

But hopefully the years
    will be a little bit
    forgiving,
'Cause challenges I'm
    sure we'll see in the

acts of daily living.

Wrinkles there will be
    galore, dentures and
    white hair,
Trusses, walkers and
    what's more, a 'scooter'
    power chair.

No doubt that we'll
    both fart and drool,
    and always make a
    stink,
And if you pee your
    pants, it's cool and
    fine by me (I think).

For to the old the
    years are kind,
    the senses they
    expose less;
Aged love's not
    only blind, but it is
    also noseless.

So, yes, it's true that
    all things end,
    and nothing lasts
    forever,
But I say to you with

love, dear friend:
"Better late than never."

—DBP Fourth of July
2023

The Ghosts of Woodstock

Back in August '69
A million* hippies did
    just fine,

Made love and very
    little harm
Way up there on
    Yasgur's farm,

Don't say Woodstock,
    that ain't right,
'Cause Bethel
    really was the site,

All the greatest sing-
    ers sang,
Their bands brought in
    by Michael Lang,

You can't say that the
    sound man stunk,
For, you see, it was
    Chip Monck,

Food from the Hog
    Farm's Wavy Gravy,
Two Monkees present:

Peter, Davy,

A psychedelic drug
    affair,
But, oddly, ShaNaNa
    were there,

One act showed timely,
    but the prize?
Rich Havens had to
    improvise,**

Kids drugged like 60s
    hippies should!
The brown acid? "Not
    too good."

And let's get straight
    on all the facts,
They had the 60s
    biggest acts,

Santana, Joplin and
    The Who,
And CCR, to name a
    few,

The hippies were not
    feeling pain
When R. Shankar played
    in the rain,

And when the end
　　came to the flood,
A hundred thousand
　　played in mud,

The kids were made
　　of hardy stuff,
At night, they had to
　　lie out rough,

But it was tough on
　　one and all
Who had to answer
　　nature's call,

For one would err
　　if one assumes
That Lang gave thought
　　to have bathrooms,

Not much sleep at
　　night achieved,
But hippie babies were
　　conceived,

No joe in morn to
　　wake them up!
Granola in a paper
　　cup!

The wake-up call that
    did the trick?
A pre-dawn set by
    Airplane's Slick,

The schedule was
    Friday-Sunday,
But music blared at
    sunup Monday,

Jimi Hendrix sang
    and played,
Die-hards sure were
    glad they stayed,

No profit was made
    but instead,
Lang was millions in
    the red,

The debt was big and
    did survive,
Right up 'til 1985,

Woodstock's long gone
    and now so's Lang,
We'll no more hear the
    songs they sang,

I wish I had been in
    that mix,
Was twenty then
    instead of six,

'Cause I have peace
    and love to spare,
Just like someone out
    of "Hair,"

A hippie's all I want
    to be:
Next lifetime maybe?
    Hey , we'll see.

—DBP 2/25/24

*actual estimate was 400,000–but rhymes gotta rhyme and meters gotta mete

**for two hours until the other bands began to arrive—he ran out of material and just started making stuff up in real time onstage—he made it interactive and the crowd loved it

Give and Take

Gen'rous is the giving
    love
With thought and word
    and deed,
It seeks not beauty,
    fame or wealth,
And giving is its
    need;

But thoughtless is the
    selfish love,
It takes when times
    are lean,
Abandons when the
    fair winds blow—
Now, don't you think
    that's mean?

—DBP 10/28/23

Giving Thanks
2024

Things are in such
    disarray
It's hard to know just
    what to say
To get in the mood
To express gratitude
As expected this
    Thanksgiving Day;

Just try give life a
    good spin,
And cover concern
    with a grin,
As you mumble
    thanks
For destiny's pranks
And make an attempt
    to fit in.

—DBP 11/28/24
    (Thanksgiving Day)

Gone

—DBP 12/12/23

Gone is the woman
    of my heart,
My teardrops fall
    like rain,
She told me that
    she must depart,
And ne'er be seen
    again,

My injured heart is
    filled with ache,
It's bruised and worn
    with care,
I fear that it must
    surely break,
From sadness and
    despair,

And as it breaks I
    wonder why
She never saw my
    worth,
I heave a last
    dejected sigh,
And sink into the
    earth.

—DBP 12/12/23

Good Writers and
Good Books

Imaginations oft insist
On making pretend
    worlds exist,

This good writers under-
    stand
When they take up
    pen in hand,

They make their realms
    like little gods,
Constructing erudite
    facades,

Wordy stages on which
    walk
Characters who live
    and talk,

Heroes save and
    villains sin,
Romance, action
    pull you in,

A play enacted on
    each page,
By players on a
    paper stage,

Castles rising from
    gray mists,
Plots that take sur-
    prising twists,

Gleaming treasures
    seekers find,
Burnished by the
    author's mind,

Good books are
    truly just as real
As how they make
    the reader feel,

And win their authors
    just renown
When you cannot put
    them down.

—DBP 7/5/25

"Grampa Sam"

by D.B. Pevney

Old Mrs. Dobrowski's old house was in the old part of old Riverhead town, Long Island, New York. It was a dingy, shabby, small two-story clapboard house on a modest lot—similar to all of the other houses on Mrs. Dobrowski's narrow street in all respects but one. Whereas every other house was flanked by two lookalike siblings, Mrs. Dobrowski's house and yard were bounded on one side by Evergreen Nondenominational Cemetery.

The grounds of the cemetery had been built up with untold tons of fill and then leveled generations ago in its preparation as a rural burial ground—with the result that the cemetery was higher by about ten feet than the neighborhood which had encroached on it from the east over the years. The boundary was a high retaining wall or bulkhead built of massive square-cut timbers, now aged and weathered, but still apparently sound.

Mrs. Dobrowski's back yard was eternally in the shadow of the close-by wooden wall—the sun never shone there and no grass grew. The long-settled black soil was bare except for patches of green lichen, a few moss-covered rocks and some stunted, straggly, anemic-looking weeds.

If you could scale the wall from Mrs. Dobrowski's back yard you would find yourself standing on the east corner of the cemetery grounds, and the first headstone you would see bore the inscription "Samuel Nussbaum January 8, 1866–March 15, 1947"

Rightly presuming that Mr. Samuel Nussbaum's casket was buried to the standard six-foot depth, and lining yourself up with his headstone while standing right next to the wall in Mrs. Dobrowski's back yard, you would be about six feet away from his remains interred just on the other side—with both of your heads (or rather, your head and his skull) on a convenient conversational level—if Mr. Nussbaum were still somehow able to talk, that is.

*   *   *   *   *   *   *   *   *

Walter Strohman was nine, and small for his age. Parentless, he was placed with the kindly but elderly widow Mrs. Dobrowski, his maternal grandmother. Walter's mother had called him Wally when she bothered to speak to him—but no one else ever did. In his short, sad life he had known indifference, neglect, abuse, impoverishment and loneliness, with a father sentenced to thirty years to life in the federal pen before Walter's first birthday, and a drug-addicted prostitute mother who had recently ended her misery by fatally overdosing.

If Walter's life was lonely before he came to live with Mrs. Dobrowski, it was no less so afterwards—at least, not at first. There were no other children on Mrs. Dobrowski's street, or on any of the neighboring streets. There hadn't been children or young adults in Mrs. Dobrowski's immediate neighborhood for years—just lonely isolated old people grimly clinging to the last of their lives, and, when they finally died, dark shuttered houses—empty for a while until furtively occupied by squatters and crackheads.

Walter's days were the same. He would wake up, get dressed, be given breakfast by Mrs. Dobrowski and then be picked up by the school bus. On the way to school, he would be picked on, bullied and ostracized. Later, in school, he would picked on, bullied and ostracized. At the end of the school day he would take the bus ride back home—and be picked on, bullied and ostracized. Little Walter's life was a series of traumas, embarrassments and miseries broken up only by periods of loneliness and boredom.

In the spring, Mrs. Dobrowski began noticing that rather than going straight to his room after school, Walter would walk out the back door, cross the shadowed back yard and go right up to the wall. On reaching it, he would pace slowly back and forth along its length. Through the back window, it looked as if he were talking to himself, although Mrs. Dobrowski couldn't make out any of the words.

The pacing and talking by the wall were an invariable routine that Walter would repeat every day as soon as he got home from school, and during most of the daylight hours on Saturdays and Sundays— stopping only to attend to essentials—getting his homework done or attending to bodily needs. The first time Mrs. Dobrowski had asked him what he was doing, he had replied, "I was talking to Grampa Sam. He's really nice and he tells me about how things were in the olden days." After that, when asked, he would answer simply "Talking to Grampa Sam" and change the subject.

Mrs. Dobrowski of course thought this behavior odd. She loved her grandson and worried that he might be suffering from some mental or emotional illness. But she had health problems of her own, and doubted that Walter's basic Medicaid would cover psychological counseling and treatment she could never pay for out of her own pocket. Even with the AFDC money she was now getting, she could barely afford necessities for the boy and herself. And besides, Walter's eccentricity was apparently harmless, and seemed to ease some of the pain he had been going through, at times making him almost cheerful. She should have such sickness, thought Mrs. Dobrowski.

The school year ended and summer began, and nothing mattered anymore to Walter except pacing the length of the wall all day long "talking to Grampa Sam." It was all Mrs. Dobrowski could do to get Walter to come inside for meals and to sleep at night.

*   *   *   *   *   *   *   *   *

One day after breakfast Mrs. Dobrowski didn't feel well. When Walter ran out the back door, she climbed the stairs with unsteady steps, holding onto the rickety banister and pausing frequently for breath. She managed to reach her bedroom and collapse on the bed, slipping in and out of consciousness.

It was later when Mrs. Dobrowski became aware of Walter yelling about something—the shade was still up on her bedroom window and she could see that it was dark out now. Walter's footsteps came banging up the steps and he burst into the room, excited and out of breath. He stood at the foot of Mrs. Dobrowski's bed.

"Gramma, Gramma guess what?" Mrs. Dobrowski had never seen Walter so animated. "Grampa Sam says he's coming to take us to stay with him. It's really nice there, much better than here. And he says we can stay there, and you can come too!"

Mrs. Dobrowski thought she heard someone else's footsteps coming up the stairs now—she could tell by the creaking of the stairs that it was a heavier tread, but it was much slower and quieter than Walter's had been.

"Gramma, he's HERE. It's Grampa Sam. C'mon get up!"

Mrs. Dobrowski saw an old man standing next to Walter at the foot of her bed. He was wearing a dark, worn suit. His features were benevolent, his expression kindly. He smiled at Mrs. Dobrowski. She smiled a faint smile in return, then closed her eyes—for the last time.

Grampa Sam took Walter by the hand and led him out of the bedroom, down the stairs and out the back door.

*   *   *   *   *   *   *   *   *

Many years later the bulkhead at the east corner of Evergreen Nondenominational Cemetery—now finally rotted through with age—gave way in a grim landslide of dirt and rocks, broken caskets and old bones.

Most of it wound up in the back yard of the old Dobrowski house, now long vacant and in a state of extreme dilapidation itself. One coffin lay on its side, contents partly spilled out.

Unaccountably, it clearly had held two sets of skeletal remains: an obviously older, arthritic adult and a small child of maybe seven years old. The casket was determined to be the one from the Samuel

Nussbaum grave—but there was no record of a child ever having been buried there.

—DBP 7/14/24

Great Fleas ("Siphonaptera")

Great fleas have litt'ler
    fleas upon their backs
    to bite 'em,
And little fleas have lesser
    fleas and so ad infinitum,

Bigger fleas themselves in
    turn have greater fleas to
    go on,
While these again have greater
    still, and greater still, and so on.

—Augustus DeMorgan

Such vermin only tease and
    pinch
Their foes still larger by an
    inch,
And naturalists observe that
    they
Have smaller fleas on them
    that prey
And these again have smaller
    ones on their backs to
    bite 'em,
And so proceed along from
    there and go ad infinitum,
And thus all poets in their

kind,
Are bit by those who come
behind.

136

—Jonathan Swift

The Green Light*

I run, I chase, I'm driven
    on, by my one desire,
An incandescence lures
    my love, a lantern to
    inspire,

Sometimes the light burns
    like the sun, and sometimes
    soft and green,
The sun is hot, and feels like
    fire, the other more serene,

Though placid is the lesser orb,
    it still allows no rest,
I soldier on without fatigue,
    I'm equal to the test,

I forge ahead and seek the
    light, whether bright or dim,
I'll never stop, I'll never tire,
    I'm sound of wind and limb,

So let me know my quest's
    not vain, not ended at its
    start,
The rest of me may fall some
    day, but never will my heart.

—DBP 6/2/25

*"The Great Gatsby"

Hachiko Haiku

So used to Mistress
The faithful dog waits the years
Loyal beyond death

—DBP 10/1/23

Hachiko

I loved you then,
    I love you now,
I'll love in 20 years
    somehow,

You like to say I
    don't know you,
And yet I know you
    through and through,

And even though
    you're far right now,
As we both breathe
    I make this vow:

The years will come,
    the years will go,
And buried deep,
    I'll just lie low,

The time will come
    my stock will rise,
My resurrection no
    surprise,

However long, the
    years I'll wait,
Love has no
    expiration date.

—DBP 12/14/23

Halloween Poem

I want to tell you all,
   my friends,
About the day October
   ends,

I eagerly await each
   fall
The raven's croak and
   eldritch call,

Then faithful will not
   hesitate,
But gather round to
   celebrate,

And revel in the darkest
   rites
Replete with many
   ghoulish sights,

A pumpkin with demonic
   mien,
And skeletons are often
   Seen,

A black cat and decrepit
   hag,
A grave-robber with spade
   and bag,

And if you listen, you can
    hear it:
The moaning of an evil
    spirit,

A wolf at yellow moon
    will howl,
And summon things even
    more foul,

Assemblages of graveyard
    rats,
Tarantulas and swooping
    bats,

Unspeakable in any terms,
Pale zombies wriggling with
    worms,

What's worse than these,
    I'd like to know?
They'd frighten Edgar
    Allan Poe!

So while I tell you
    to beware,
If you are up for a
    good scare,

It's very simple as you
  see:
Just pick your phone up
  and call me!

—DBP 7/8/23

Hamsters

Today the hamster
    gets a nod—
This creature is a
    little odd,

The thing's a fat and
    fluffy fur ball,
But sans a tail like
    cousin gerbil,

I don't know where
    they come from
    really,
They're found at pet
    stores most ideally,

Just keep one 'cause
    two might fight,
And pet 'em careful—
    they sometimes
    bite,

And please get them a
    running wheel
To make them fit and
    healthy feel,

It keeps them active
    and not lazy
Although the noise can
    drive you crazy,

And water in a tube
    of glass
For every hamster
    lad and lass,

Please feed 'em pellets,
    leafy stuff
'Cause they can never
    get enough,

As moms to babies
    you can't beat 'em
(Except when they
    decide to eat 'em*)

You keep 'em in a tank
    or cage,
The ideal pet at any
    age,

And your pennies you
    should save
To buy a nesting box
    or cave—

They really like to
    be secure,
They need that
    safe place to be
    sure,

I think that's what
    you need to know
To make your hamster
    thrive and grow,

But if they die of
    hamster pox,
Just stuff 'em in
    an old shoe box.

—DBP 5/3/24

(*They sometimes eat
their babies for no
known reason.)

A Happy Thought

There is always lots of
    work,
And lots of chances then
    to shirk,
One time when I was
    mowing grass
Allowing wand'ring
    thoughts to pass
Like graceful spirits
    of the air,
On looking down I
    had a care—
For there sprawled
    out upon the lawn
A work of art and color
    drawn
By happiness and joy
    in life,
And vanished then all
    weary strife,
I helped it loft into
    the air
To save itself and me
    from care,
But then it topped the
    trees, was gone,
And I in wonder looking
    on

Knew then as I surely
    ought,
The flying of a happy
    thought.

—DBP 9/8/24

The Hill, the Creek
and the Dog in
March

Behind my house there's
   lots of trees
With branches rustling in
   breeze.
I look, my heart begins
   to sing
Even though it's early
   spring.
Not so thick with fol-
   iage yet,
The ground is soggy
   and rain-wet.
But the conifers are
   green,
All-in-all a pleasant
   scene.
Though it's downhill
   my pace will slack-
   en
To get through all that
   scratchy bracken.
Yet go I must, o'er
   root and log,
To get my widely
   wand'ring dog.

And she must get a
    close-up look
At the burbling creek
    (or, brook?)
Which runs along the
    bottom there,
Very near a fox's lair.
And she is tranced with
    every smell
Which works on her it's
    magic spell—
She listens for a splash
    or two
To get a jumping frog-
    gy view.
But I must fetch her
    and beware,
And take her up away
    from there,
For in the shadows and
    the murk
Coyote or hunter there
    may lurk.
And so I chase her with
    a will,
And leash and take her
    up the hill.
I make the climb back
    up and then
I'm out of breath and

home again.
I'm scratched and sore,
    my knees both hurt,
I'm sweaty and I tore my
    shirt.
I'll nurse my injuries in
    sorrow,
But do it all again
    tomorrow!

—DBP 3/16/24

His Poetry

He lends his pen
    to thoughts of her
    that flow from it
    in solitude,
For he's her poet,
    and she his
    poetry.

—Dedication by Lang
    Leav, rewrite by
    DBP 12/18/24

The House in
Summer

The house is pretty all
    year round,
But summer's when it's
    beauty's crowned,

Each leaf and flower,
    bloom and vine
Strive their beauty to
    combine,

And pretty little
    creatures there,
Deer and squirrel and
    summer hare,

Likewise put on quite
    a show,
As if they wanted you
    to know

How very nice the place
    can be:
The house is summer, you
    and me.

—DBP 6/17/24

Hypatia

World renowned for
   grace and wit,
She was learning's
   favorite,

Philosopher both sage
   and wise,
Her thought rejecting
   mere surmise,

She kept good science
   in her sight,
And by the way, she
   sure could write,

A she-scholar among
   the men,
Unmatched when she
   took up the pen,

Her study habits down-
   right scary,
She lived inside the
   Great Library,*

One day she grew to
   be too smart,
And envy bloomed in
   every heart,

She was then mobbed
    and much abused
With hatred that the
    men enthused,

Her wisdom they could
    not forgive,
She couldn't be allowed
    to live,

They pelted her with
    shells and stones,
And tore the flesh right
    off her bones,

In agony she bled and
    died,
But her fame lived and
    traveled wide,

And it goes on even
    today,
Nor to dim or fade
    away,

So long as wisdom
    honor gives,
So long it is
    Hypatia lives.

—DBP 5/4/24

*Of Alexandria, repository of all
scholarship and knowledge of the
ancient world.

I Love Her

I love her for her depth
    of soul,
I love her for her spirit,
As long as I am on a
    roll,
I think she ought to
    hear it—

She's the one whom I
    adore,
And this there's no
    denying,
And if she needs hear
    any more,
I'll surely keep on
    trying. 😊 💜

—DBP 4/5/25

I Dreamt of Mike

I dreamt of Mike. We were side by side, chatting contentedly while walking. This was in the downtown area of some nice Long Island town. We were passing by stores and restaurants. Sidewalks, manicured trees, tended grass—Huntington or maybe Garden City. It was a bright, sunny, blue sky day—warm but not hot, with a slight breeze—later morning maybe, before lunchtime. Very pleasant. We were in jeans, T-shirts, sneakers. He was young, but not at his heaviest. Closer to 200 lbs than 300, but not gaunt. Features not sharp or pinched-looking. Unreceded hairline, no gray. He was happy, energetic, and was setting a vigorous walking pace. He seemed fine, talking quite a bit like he used to do, not out of breath at all.

I said, "Mike, the entire time I've known you, you've been a law student or a lawyer. I can't even imagine you doing anything else. What are you going to do now?"

He at first answered, "I don't know." But he seemed untroubled by that.

He seemed to be about to discuss the possibilities, but first had an aside about how Laura was doing. He started saying something about that.

Then I awoke.

—DBP 11/16/23

I Fled You

I fled you, down the nights and down the
days,

I fled you, through the arches of the
years,

I fled you, down the labyrinthine ways

Of my own mind, in a mist of tears.

from " The Hound of Heaven"
by Francis Thompson, 1890

I'm a Lawyer

I use oratorical
  force,
On topics both
  genteel and
  coarse,
And dispute with
  a will
While I never keep
  still,
So I'm often
  consid'rably
  hoarse.

—DBP 7/1/24

I'm the Guy

When I'm forced down
   to my knees,
I know someone is hard
   to please,

And when my heart with
   pain's beset,
I know someone plays
   hard to get,

And when I look, what do
   I see?
A frustrating reality,

I'm a poet, literary,
In Latin too—now that
   is scary,

I'm ro-man-TIC as
   Ro-me-O
(I've affidavits, so
   you know),

I am creative, can
   invent,
Practice law to pay
   the rent,

I have ingenuity and
    spirit—
If you're impressed
    I'd like to hear it,

Love animals and
    nature too,
But most important:
    I LOVE YOU,

Your indifference?
    Hard for me,
But for you too a
    tragedy'

So never ask, don't
    wonder why,
I hope you get it:
    I'M THE GUY.

—DBP 7/29/24

I'm There

This love endures
    the decades long,
Proving smug pre-
    diction wrong,

And it will ever be
    this way,
My thoughts about you
    every day

Go out across each
    hour and mile
Swiftly flying all the
    while,

A blurred trajectory
    of speed
But scant relief to
    far-off need,

For while I'm with you
    in a blink,
A shadow's all I am,
    I think,

Mere efforts on one side
    to heal,
That question whether
    you can feel,

But I love so hard you
    see,
I can't help hoping you
    sense me.

—DBP 7/13/24

Ides of March

I wonder if it's now too
    late?
A time for bigots and
    for hate?
I struggle now so I
    can see
A little shred of
    decency,
Well, it's still there
    if you but look,
Not everyone's an
    asshole crook,
I'll not cave in, but
    bide my time,
Although I know not
    every crime
Will reap its due, and
    so it goes,
We waste our time who
    weep our woes,
The only way to set it
    right,
Is rise above and bring
    the fight,
And I'll die happy, I'll
    die well,
If I drag them all to
H**l

—DBP 3/15/25

Maybe, in the end, all
that matters is the fight,
even if you cannot win—
there's always something
to be said for going down
in flames—history tends to
remember and revere her
flaming assholes 🔥

Ides

They mark some things
    besides
Our yearly springward
    strides,
I raise a full cup
To poets, my pup*
I really do like the Ides.

—DBP 1/13/25

*March 21 is usually first
day of Spring, and it's
World Poetry Day and
Diana's reported birthday
(March 21, 2020). Ides of
March are actually March
15–poetic license!

If Wishes Were Fishes

If wishes were fishes,
    then beggars would ride,
If turnips were watches,
    I'd wear one at my side,
If "ifs" and "ands" were
    pots and pans,
There's be no work for
    tinkers' hands.

—Traditional

In Our Youth

In our youth we knew magic,
Breathed fire,
Sang of heroes.
Now shadows of things long departed,
Dead ghosts,
Walk among us in silent mockery,
Inmates of a gray world.

—DBP 9/30/22

In Over My Head *

In Rincón on one sunny
    day,
The dolphins beckoned
    me to play,

So my pirata** in my
    hand,
I swam to sea and quit
    the land,

My cutoff jeans were
    all I wore,
As I left behind the
    shore,

No jet-ski, surfboard,
    water wings,
No safety gear or
    suchlike things,

The water was two
    fathoms deep,
What fate for rashness
    would I reap?

In truth I'm at home in
    the water,
Sometimes I think I'm
    partly otter,***

I bobbed at sea and
     sipped my rum,
Not worried about
     what might come,

Cool water soothed
     my drunken pate,
And happy I did not
     fear fate,

The land was a ten
     minute's swim
When I first caught
     sight of him,

Fins five feet from
     tail to dorsal,****
To him I'd be a rum-
     soaked morsel!

I didn't panic, not
     much point—
I'd soon be torn from
     limb to joint,

Might as well enjoy
     my drink
Before my bloody
     bones would sink,

And so I took a swig
    of rum,
And contemplated
    Kingdom Come,

But Jaws was in a
    pensive mood,
With no wish that
    day to intrude,

He circled in a lazy
    arc
That left me puzzled,
    in the dark,

And all at once I
    was aware,
About me that shark
    didn't care,

And not a nibble did
    he take
(Perhaps he had a
    stomach-ache?)

And though it's odd
    I have to think
That as he left he
    gave a wink,

And flashed at me a
toothy grin
To show the danger
I'd been in,

I swam to land, more
sad than wise,
Because I came to
realize

That if I really was
so great,
How quickly then I'd
have been ate,

But since I really
didn't matter,
I wasn't on shark's
dinner platter.

—DBP 5/6/24

*A 100% true story!

**A full-sized coconut with most of the milk drained off and
filled back up to the top with rum, splash of lime optional.

***I really am a good ocean swimmer—give me a pair of fitted
swim fins and I'll give a whale a run for its money.

**** This equals a ten-foot shark.

In the Final Analysis

In the final analysis,
Love—anyone's love
For anyone—is a
Mystery.
Who can fathom the
Depth of Love?
Who can understand its
True nature?
The truth is that
Love was never meant to
Analyzed at all. It was and
Is only to be felt.

—DBP Fall 2021

Inkwell, a V-Day Poem

What's a poet sans a
    muse?
Why write if you do
    not enthuse?

How then make your
    verses dance?
And to what point
    without romance?

The beating heart is
    your wellspring,
Your passion will the
    verses bring;

Without that, writing's
    just a drudge,
A long and sweetly
    sticky trudge;

But when love's true,
    it will abide,
You'll never put the
    pen aside.

—DBP 2/14/25

Insomnia

Once more you're in
    trouble deep,
It's 3:00 AM and you
    can't sleep,

All kinds of thoughts
    come rushing in,
What you've done and
    where you've been,

Problems faced by our
    whole nation,
The entire global
    situation,

Money, family—lots
    of cares
Just sneak up on
    you unawares,

Could it have been
    something you ate?
Perhaps if you just
    masturbate?

Well, that was fun but
    didn't work,
And now you feel like
    such a jerk,

You try some more, but
    thoughts still race,
A hectic look comes
    on your face,

Then swirling thoughts
    start to align,
You start to think things
    may be fine,

You grab a paper scrap
    and pen,
Immerse yourself in
    scribbling then,

You scrawl and scratch
    for good or ill,
No going back—it's
    seized your will,

The stanzas come both
    thick and fast,
The verses fly from
    first to last,

Then comes the dawn
    and morning light
And it's all down in
    black and white,

A triumph of the
    written word,
Or maybe just a
    rhyming turd,

It matters not, this
    much is true:
Again you've done
    that thing you do,

Now bleary-eyed you
    stretch and yawn,
Blink in the pale light
    of dawn,

Who cares if night's
    now at an end?
Insomnia's the poet's
    friend!

—DBP 2/11/24

Insomnia Too

Don't ask about all my
  dark fears,
Or why late at night I
  shed tears,
The reasons, you see,
That overcame me
Are what everybody
  now hears—

The future we never
  foresaw,
With kleptocrats out-
  side the law,
Has murdered my
  sleep—
And top of the
  heap
Sits an orange, devour-
  ing maw.

—DBP 10/24/24

Insomniac Writer

Of all of those who
   REM sleep lack,
I am the king
   insomniac,

While others lie in bed
   asnore,
I go about my nightly
   chore,

Happy nighttime naps
   they take,
While all the while I'm
   wide awake,

And on my wordy nightly
   quest,
This weary writer gets
   no rest,

At times I'm calm, at
   times I'm wired,
Or wide awake, or just
   plain tired,

I don't do it for fame or
   glory,
Just for a poem or short
   story,

The work can stall, I
    will admit,
And oftentimes the
    product's s**t,

But sometimes when
    it comes out great,
Then it's OK I stayed up
    late,

Next day I'll stumble
    through my morn,
Coffee-buzzed, dazed
    and forlorn,

I'll look at what I wrote
    last night
To see if it came out
    alright,

And maybe then I'll
    see it's good,
That now I will be
    understood,

And as I lift my
    coffee cup,
It seems my soul
    is lifted up,

Then reading on with
    bleary eyes,
I all too sudden
    realize

That good or bad it
    matters not—
No one will read a
    single jot,

Now wide-awake I get
    a grip:
I haven't any reader-
    ship

—DBP 5/25/24

Inspiration

Whenever I am down,
I think about you dear,
And soon I cease to
    frown,
And sadness turns to
    cheer,

The idea of you so
    sweet,
It makes good feelings
    grow,
You sweep me off my
    feet,
You make endorphins
    flow,

At mention of your name,
My thoughts are never
    barren,
None other is the same
As exalted, lovely 'Karen'

Just hearing it inspires,
Calls forth both pad and
    pen,
My muse but rarely tires,
Then coffee, and off again,

The results are quite a mix,
To this I must confess,
But I labor on to fix
Each rhyming, metric mess,

My sweet how you uplift
   me!
With you I'm never bored,
Love for you will always
   be
My poetical reward!

—DBP 6/30/23

Intimations of Mortality

A buried memory may
   steal,
Intrude on happy moments
   few,
And ancient wounds you'd
   thought to heal,
Begin to sting and bleed
   anew,

Thus for always death-
   less pain,
Our hurts may fade
   but never die,
And hopes once bright
   now seem in vain,
We shake our heads
   and wonder: Why?

We cry
Our tears
For all
Our years
Rush toward
Our ends
As welcome
Friends

—DBP 5/31/24

Intimations of Immortality
(Exerpts)

There was a time when meadow, grove, and stream,
The earth, and every common sight,
       To me did seem
      Apparelled in celestial light,
The glory and the freshness of a dream.
It is not now as it hath been of yore;—
       Turn wheresoe'er I may,
        By night or day.
The things which I have seen I now can see no more.

Whither is fled the visionary gleam?
Where is it now, the glory and the dream?

Our birth is but a sleep and a forgetting:
The Soul that rises with us, our life's Star,
       Hath had elsewhere its setting,
       And cometh from afar:
       Not in entire forgetfulness,
       And not in utter nakedness,
But trailing clouds of glory do we come
       From God, who is our home:
Heaven lies about us in our infancy!
Shades of the prison-house begin to close
       Upon the growing boy.

—William Wordsworth

Jazz Love

Soft jazz in the City
	night,
The fire casts a
	trancing light,

The radio's on and
	plays Coltrane,
To Johnny Hartman's
	sad refrain,*

The cozy factor's off
	the charts,
Contentment in two
	beating hearts,

One martini's one
	too few,
But who cares since
	I love you.

—DBP 6/2/24

*"Lush Life"
	Coltrane/Hartman

Karma

Justice comes in many
    shapes,
But from its ends no
    one escapes,

Observe the irony
    that's in it,
And please give ear
    for just a minute:

A rich man revels in his
    wealth,
And yet he suffers from
    poor health,

And to the faithless it
    is meet
That their own loved ones
    also cheat,

Gluttons' portliness they
    flout,
But corpulence makes hearts
    give out,

And who by cleverness is
    ruled,
Will see that it's himself
    he's fooled,

But callous friends are worst
    of all,
For them is saved the
    hardest fall,

'Cause those who push true
    friends away
Will live on to a bitter day,

And linger toward a
    lonely end,
And friend-depriving, have
    no friend.

—DBP 9/21/23

Keeping the Path

I keep the path open
    to you,
Cutting back weeds
    when I'm blue,
Against the sure day
I've gone the whole way,
And happy I finally
    got through.

—DBP 8/18/24

Keeping Your Interest

While future love can
    be quite real,
It hasn't got a solid
    feel,

It may seem a bit
    tenuous
(Not being disingen-
    uous)

And so I do what-
    e'er I can,
Solidify my noble
    plan,

I keep it light, don't
    get too deep,
In hopes your interest
    I can keep.

—DBP 5/10/25

Kor's Remonstrance

"Savor the fruit of life my young friends;
It has a sweet taste when it is fresh from the vine.
But don't live too long;
The taste grows bitter after a time."

—from "Once More Unto the Breach"
Star Trek Deep Space Nine 7.7
written by Ronald D. Moore

Law and Poetry

Lawyering's a noble trade,
The profession second
    oldest,

Practitioners aren't born,
    they're made,
But success goes to the
    boldest.

Courtroom battles oft
    excite,
And trials get quite heated,

But when doing paperwork
    at night,
Something else is needed.

My mind then wanders, and
    my pen
Away from law and strife.

So is it any wonder then,
I ruminate on life?

Emotions, thoughts and
    lofty themes,
I strive to feel and know 'em,

The way to do that best,
   it seems,
Is to put them in a poem.

And this is why I'll ne'er
   become
Another Clarence Darrow,

Won't follow every rule of
   thumb,
Stay on the straight and
   narrow,

But waste my talents and
   my time,
And risk censure, dirty
   looks

Reducing all to silly
   rhyme,
For putting in my books.

—DBP 7/9/23

The Lemmings

Lemmings are small creatures,
mammals, warm-blooded.
The females nurse their babies.
They live in large social groups.
In each group, a leader will emerge,
a large, aggressive male,
no more intelligent than the rest.
Not rational, but rather functioning
on instinct, which can be defective.
This lemming will sometimes
decide on something for the group.
He will lead them to the edge
of a cliff and jump off.
For the others, there is no
thought, no dissent,
no whys or wherefores.
They must follow, blindly.
And so they jump—males,
females, babies—thoughtlessly plunging
And dying, all dying.
But there's no need to ask
what lemmings are.
We are lemmings.—March 2023

Let Poesy be First, or Petronius on
the Proper Way to Teach Young Men
(yes, it's sexist) to be Poets*

"Whether to Tritonia's famous halls
The Muses lead his steps, or to those walls
That Spartan exiles rear'd or where
The Sirens' song thrill'd the enraptured air
Of all his tasks let Poesy be first,
And Homer's verse the fount to quench his thirst.
Soon will he master deep Socratic lore,
And wield the arms Demosthenes erst bore.
Then to new modes must he in turn be led,
And Grecian wit to Roman accents wed.
Nor in the forum only will he find
Meet occupation for his busy mind;
On books he'll feast, the poet's words of fire,
Heroic tales of war and Tully's patriot ire,
Such be thy studies; then, whate'er the theme,
Pour forth thine eloquence in copious stream."

*From "The Satyricon" by Petronius, translation
attributed to Oscar Wilde

Let's Live and Love

I've said I love you,
And you love me too,
But you think our love
    fails every test,

So just what's the sense
Of intransigence?
Why not let it die and go
    rest?

Well, that just won't do,
I'll explain it to you,
If you'll give an ear to my
    speech,

Do my best to tell
What you know
    so well,
While staying outside
    of my reach,

Email, text and phone—
I don't feel alone,
With means my loving
    to convey,

And making the most
Of good old U.S. Post

Speeds my loving notes
    on their way,

Wish we could embrace,
I'd kiss your sweet face,
So often I pray this could
    be,

But without these things
My old heart still sings,
You seem very close
    now to me,

I'll sing the same song
To last my life long,
And never get tired
    or falter,

No adverse event
Can make any dent,
Or cause my affections
    to alter,

I won't let love go,
It'll just thrive and
    grow,
As sure as there's
    a God above,

Love lives, it is
        true,
So I say now to you:
Beloved, just lets
        live and love.

—DBP 12/9/24

Library Fun

A day at the library's fun,
While perhaps a bit lacking in sun,
But I note with some glee,
When it's Karen and me,
My happiness comes by the ton.

—DBP 6/10/23

Library Lady

She seeks out the less
    trodden ways, among
    the shelves and stacks,
The volumes are her
    closest friends, no
    company she lacks,

And often through the
    gloomy days she sits
    in quiet rooms,
Delights in peace and
    quietude of literary
    tombs,

She loves to read, and
    while her writing
    efforts have been slight,
She'll sometimes take a
    pen in hand and sad
    sweet poems write,

The way she loves seems
    strange to me, but who
    cares how it looks
That she's the type who'll
    often shun the people
    for the books,

In life it's sometimes
    difficult for our true
    paths to see,
But for her the way is
    always clear: it's to
    the library.

—DBP 11/19/23

Life and Death

I hear beneath the life
    I've had
A soundtrack sweet and
    kind of sad,

And see the road, all ruts
    and curves,
Remembering the stops
    and swerves,

And driving rain and
    ceaseless strife
Which oddly framed
    the joys of life,

I know not where that
    life will tend,
But I'm not ready for
    the end,

And when I reach it, I
    will see
What's beyond that
    end for me,

So I'll just shrug and
    hope my best
That darkness comes,
    I'll get some rest.

—DBP 5/31/25

Life Is Messy

It seems we all run toward
    a goal
That's built upon
    quicksand
And everybody plays a role
And none can understand

That perfect life will
    never be
And, no, you can't have
    peace
For always problems you
    will see
And strife without
    surcease

Health crises, kids and
    finance woes
And always death and taxes
Relationships complex, God
    knows
The angst never relaxes

You'll find the key to
    maintain calm
Is a little gallows cheer
So mount the scaffold
    with aplomb
And never shed a tear

—DBP 9/1/23

Life Unlived, A, or,
The Inner Light

I live a life of duty, law—
    I think I live it well.
But once I had an almost-life,
    and of this I must tell:

I never had that other life,
    but yet again I did,
And of it there are memories,
    which from my mind are
    hid,

I had a wife, a home, a
    place—a loving family,
And even now I think
    sometimes that time
    could almost be,

I lived and loved and
    laughed and cried,
    and played some
    music sweet,
Now all I do is weep
    and mourn the
    almost-time's defeat,

For now that time can
    never come, which

in that dream-life
   could,
And if it were to come
   today, well what would
   be the good?

For times of dreams are
   gone and done, as
   soon as we awake,
And never can be lived
   again for someone
   else's sake,

And yes, I have my love,
   my love, and it will never
   die,
But wishing for it to be
   real will only make me
   cry.

—DBP 1/30/24

Light in Darkness

Dark is dark and black
    is black, or so it's
    often said,
But I know of a brighter dark
    that comes to me instead,

I see it when I visit with the
    fairy lady green,
The love of art's insanity,
    the madman poet's
    queen,

Her magic from the worm-
    wood comes, in brush and
    bracken rough,
Distilled down to an essence,
    a small glass is enough,

Her taste is somewhat bitter
    so her suitors will perfuse
Her spirit sweetly through a
    lump of sugar which they
    use,

It mixes with the ice-water,
    pale emerald and opaque,
Louching this is called and
    then it's time the drink to
    take,

And when the darkness starts
    to fall her lovers feel alright,
For always in the darkness
    comes the radiant green
    light.

—DBP 11/18/23

Limburger
Limerick

I quoted an old rule
    of thumb,
But K's shy muse
    wouldn't come—
When it comes to the poems,
And all that we owe 'em,
We are both just depressingly
    dumb.

—DBP Fall/Winter 2022

Limerick

The limerick packs laughs
   anatomical
Into space that is quite
   economical,
But the good ones I've
   seen
Are so seldom clean,
And the clean ones are
   so seldom comical.

—Anon

A Loaf of Bread, a
Jug of Wine and Thou

I remember the day
You picked me up
From that damp and
Flooded rented room;
We had a diner breakfast,
Went to the library,
Happily roaming the
Shelves; we picked out
Books and sat in the
Comfy chairs; we read,
But I dozed too. After
That we went to the
Park, reclining in
Forbidden grass; we
Read some more;
Wrote poetry a bit;
We were lying down,
Looking up at the
Tree we were under,
Leaves, branches, sky.
I had a torn flannel
Shirt, rolled up for a
Pillow; you rested your
Head on my left
Shoulder, nestling into
Me a little—So nice! So
Comfortable! So happy!

I would live in that
Moment, die in it,
Stay in it
Forever.

—DBP 7/9/23

Lost and Found

I had you and a fool I
  tossed
My love and then my
  love was lost,

And soon I came to
  rue the day
I let my love just slip
  away,

Then decades passed
  but not all well
(Sometimes it was just
  like Hell)

But Fate will sometimes
  wonders give,
So happy I that I
  should live

To find you once again
  at last
In spite of all the years
  that passed,

And though it's true that
  you're not mine,
You're back (or I am)—
  I feel fine!

—DBP 4/27/24

Lost Love

I think of you all through
    the years that go to
    make lost loves,
And feel a pang inside
    my heart since
    thinking little proves,

But blessed sunshine
    smiles on me remem-
    bering your face,
And though you may not
    be with me, you're
    still in my embrace.

—DBP 1/3/25

Love Is

With love, it's never a
question about what
you want or don't
want, what's convenient,
what makes sense,
what fits in your life,
what's best for you.
Love is an unexplain-
able intangible.
It isn't there,
then it is—
forever.

—DBP 6/15/24

Love is Blue

Love is blue it always
   seems,
And unrequited haunts
   my dreams,

With such longing I'm
   not sure
If there can ever be a
   cure,

I hurt and weep and pine
   and trudge
Through life so sadly—
   what a drudge!

I sing my songs and
   every word
Despairs of ever
   being heard,

There's no relief that
   life can bring—
So melancholy is
   my thing!

—DBP 12/7/24

Love Is Messy

When someone feels true
    love inside he
Knows it isn't neat and
    tidy,

Kind of like an unmade
    bed
(Or pigeons crapping on
    your head)

And worse, a genuine
    torch song
Goes on and on his
    whole life long,

And without guile or
    collusion,
He's forced to reach
    this one conclusion:

That to avoid a lot of
    stress he
Must accept that love
    is messy.

—DBP 8/17/24

Love Is
Uncomfortable

The intensest loves of
    all do not for comfort
    make,
They upset plans and
    lives, and give less
    than they take,

With moments which
    elate, and others
    fraught with fear,
Embarrassments galore,
    worth every pain and
    tear.

—DBP 2/10/24

Love Letters

We've exchanged both
   poems and prose
With lilac verse in order-
   ed rows

That with such endear-
   ments drip
Off the tongue and o'er
   the lip

Like sugar syrup from
   a jar
Such sticky stuff will
   take you far

And line on line of
   sweetness cloys
With such pretty
   rhyming noise

And yet as silly
   as this seems
It serves to bare our
   deepest dreams

Cause pen on paper
   makes so clear
The thoughts of you my
   heart holds dear

And if forgetful take
       the pen
And scribble life in
       love again

Thus you can know
       I'll e'er love you
And never reason give
       to rue

And thus I know that
       you love me
(though I must jog
       your memory!)

—DBP 10/13/23

Love, Marriage and Divorce, a Tale of Real-Life Tragedy in Eight Words, Which Is Considerably Less Words Than Its Title Has

Fated

Dated

Waited

'Bated

Mated

Sated

Berated

Hated

—The End—

—DBP 7/23/25

Love or Communism

They say love's patient and
it's kind.
And many say it's also
blind.

True lovers see the common
good,
As everybody knows they
should.

They contribute what they
can afford,
Each one gives and no one
hoards.

But what is this
philosophy?
What is the basis we
can see?

True, Cupid's arrow flies
with sparks,
But in the end we get
Karl Marx.

—DBP 7/1/23

Mad Poets Society

A little crazy's good
   for verse,
Cold logic only makes
   it worse,

And if you want to be
   a hit,
Let your eyes spin just
   a bit,

Heavy thinking kills the
   flow,
Nobody cares how much
   you know,

All good poets keep it
   real
Not by knowledge but
   by feel,

So when you put your
   pen to pad,
By all means be a
   little mad,

The world right now is
   in a mess,
So write with all your
   craziness!

—DBP 6/14/24

Mad Poets

You and I are quite
  a pair,
Both off the beaten
  path my dear,

I've got baggage, so
  have you,
But that's OK, most
  people do,

I don't know if we'll
  live to see
Our compatibility,

That makes me blue,
  but I console
Myself with wordy
  folderol,

That we both love
  the written word
Is something all our
  friends have
  heard,

And working with a
  few loose screws,
Makes the life easy
  to choose,

Cheer up therefore,
    and don't be sad—
All poets are a little
    mad!

—DBP 12/4/23

Mailing It In

Long distance can limit
    the chances
For lovers pursuing
    romances,
Which partly explains
The mellifluous strains
Of my purple prosaic
    advances;

I'll admit that I'm not
    always smiles
At a distance of six
    hundred miles,
But I'm patient and
    kind
In my heart and my
    mind,
As I exercise metrical
    wiles.

—DBP 12/5/24

Martian Blues

Let's rocket ourselves
    to the stars,
And go on a day-trip
    to Mars,
We'll have a quick
    nip
At the end of the
    trip
'Cause the Martians
    have really great
    bars;

We'll drink while the
    sky overhead,
Turns from pink to a
    dark shade of red,
And it can be seen
That the bartender's
    green
With bright yellow spots
    on his head;

We'll sit at the bar as
    we muse,
While sipping some
    strong purple booze,
Then get in a funk
As we slowly get drunk

To the sound of some
  weird Martian blues.

—DBP 12/23/24

Memories are
Ghosts

Memories are ghosts
   you know,
Sometimes they have
   no tact to show,
They can haunt or
   they can soothe,
And sometimes give you
   simple truth.

And yet it's also
   true they lie,
The wisest could not
   tell you why,
They cheat and often
   just dissemble—
No, they're not a sacred
   temple.

Reality was what
   was then,
But another's made
   just when
You call to mind but
   through your lens,
Your psyche alters
   and amends,

Sometimes for good,
    sometimes for bad,
Depending on the life
    you've had.
I'll trust them to my
    dying day;
But worth that trust?
    Well, who can say.

As spirits go they're
    slippery,
And full of mist
    and frippery,
Such wily ghosts
    they are for sure,
You just don't know
    if they are pure.

But pure or not, I
    look to mine,
All wavy-edge and
    no clear line,
And I will always
    wish it so,
'Cause if they're false,
    don't want to know.

So let the little
    ghosties haunt,
And take me on a

pleasant jaunt—
I see my loves all
    young and fair,
No wrinkled faces,
    no gray hair,

And I am always
    young and strong,
And brave and smart
    and never wrong.
With memories like
    these you see,
I always get the best
    of me.

—DBP 2/26/24

Memory or Dream?

I remember brightness,
   energy, enthusiasm,
I remember a smile, flash
   of white teeth, a gleam
   in the eye and a dimpled
   cheek,
I remember a sea-foam of
   black curls,
I remember liveliness, playful-
   ness,
I remember a wonderful
   voice for speaking and
   singing,
I remember a laugh that
   made me laugh too,
I remember silliness for
   its own sake,
I remember passion.
Sometimes it seems
   like it was two years
   ago, and sometimes
   like it was two centuries.
And sometimes it seems
   like it never really
   happened at all,
That it's just a dream
   I dreamt
Long ago.

—DBP 3/18/24

Messages in
Bottles

Why is it I write and
    mail,
And never quit and
    never fail?

I post-card what I
    want to say,
A notes-in-bottles
    castaway,

A run a happy post-card
    shop,
And nevermore intend
    to stop,

My lost love was a
    blow for sure,
But mailing cards is
    quite the cure,

Do you put them in
    a stash?
Or simply dump them
    in the trash?

Oh well, if thrown away
    they go,

It matters not—I'll
    never know,

But the latter would
    be sad, you see,
'Cause someday they'll
    be worth money!

—DBP 2/13/24

Miss Priss

Penelope Priss,
Her mind is amiss!
Alack and alas,
She's a pain in the
  ass!
So I'll just have to
  give her a kiss 😙

—DBP 6/24/25

The Monster and
the Creature
(A Love Poem
of Halloween)

It was a dark and stormy
    night,
And in the tower high,
In a ghoulish nightmare
    lab,
The monster heaved a
    sigh,

He was fully eight feet
    tall,
And strong as any giant,
But just the doctor's
    mindless slave,
So captive and compliant,

Chained up to an oaken
    board,
Raised at an awkward
    slant,
He viewed the scene
    spread out before,
A wretched revenant,

The doctor toiled and
  worked away
In that creepy tomb,
And he made it night
  and day
An operating room,

For covered over by a
  sheet,
A form did therein lie,
The monster peered and
  tried in vain,
But naught could he
  espy

On what the doctor
  worked so hard
But one day it did
  chance
The doctor took the
  sheet away,
The monster caught a
  glance,

And right away he was
  enthralled,
His eyes beheld a
  vision
Of beauty in each jagged
  scar,
Of grace in each incision,

You and I would look
Upon that horror with
    a fright,
But to the monster then
    and there
It was love at first sight!

Her bloodshot eyes they
    did look out,
And then their gazes
    met,
The monster's mighty
    heart leapt up,
His destiny was set,

He'd love her far and
    love her near,
Forever and a day,
And nothing ever would
    befall
To take this love
    away,

But was the mad old
    doctor pleased?
Did his heart leap and
    sing?
No—something tragic had
    gone wrong,
And would misfortune
    bring,

The doc then he became
  unhinged,
His faculties derailed
Because it seemed to
  him right then
His experiment had
  failed,

But then he got under
  control,
His emotions all were
  placid,
And then he threw a
  big lever,
Dumped the creature
  into acid,

She never screamed at
  all or thrashed,
And her composure kept,
She didn't make the slight-
  est sound,
But grievous tears she
  wept,

And as she slowly sank
  way down
Into the sizzling vat,
The monster's eyes
  again found hers,

And quickly that was
    that,

The monster then he
    roared in rage,
And snapped his chains
    like thread,
The doctor then he tried
    to run,
But knew that he was
    dead,

The monster quickly
    cornered him,
And with scary monster
    power,
Grabbed him by his
    scrawny throat
And flung him from the
    tower,

The doctor in slow-
    motion fell,
For what seemed like
    a night,
He felt the mortal
    anguish and
A stomach-heaving
    fright,

He plummeted through
      rain-drenched sky
As lightning lit the
      black,
In terror did regret he
      caused
The monster to attack,

That crazy doctor fell
      and fell,
And spun himself
      around,
And with a grisly
      ghastly thump
He finally hit the
      ground,

His vertebrae they
      all were cracked,
His bones they all
      were shattered,
His skull was smashed
      and broke apart,
His brains they all
      were splattered,

The tragic monster
      was bereft,
His life was at an
      end,

He'd lost his true and
    only love,
He'd lost his dearest
    friend,

And then he ripped into
    his chest,
Rending flesh and bone,
For he preferred to bleed
    and die
Than to live on alone,

He really made a bloody
    mess
As long as he was
    able,
And with his final,
    dying breath
Slammed something on
    the table,

It was the strangest
    thing of all
E'er known in love or
    art,
On inspection what
    they found:
*A BLOODY BEATING
    HEART.*

Happy Halloween

—DBP 4/10/24

The Mourner of
Lost Years

I remember, I remember, I
    remember still
The years on years that did
    their work, and did just
    what they will,

It matters not, no difference
    makes, and never will at all,
For what will be, what was and
    is—all at my beck and
    call,

So travel'd I the years and lives
    and as it seemed, with ease,
And never bent the knee at
    all the decades to appease,

But not for joy did I these
    things, nor ease of heart
    or mind,
I did them out of fealty to
    laws of love that bind,

And finish in observing that
    it IS a cursed spite,
That my sad fate's to mourn
    lost years impossible to
    right.

—DBP 6/25/24

Nature of Love 1

In the final analysis,
Love—anyone's love
For anyone—is a
Mystery.
Who can fathom the
Depth of Love?
Who can understand its
True nature?
The truth is that
Love was never meant to
Analyzed at all. It was and
Is only to be felt.

—DBP Fall 2021

Nature of Love 2

Could be sometimes you're
    on the fence,
And can't see any recom-
    pense—
True love is volitional,
Not always positional,
And oftentimes makes
    little sense.

—DBP 5/10/25

Happy New Year 2026

No years's all good, no
    year's all bad,
And each year will beget
Some times happy, some
    times sad,
And some with angst
    beset;

We've done our best
    —was it enough?
Or must we now regret?
Some things went smooth
    and some went rough—
It's time for a re-set;

And so I pray the Fates
    right now
Our happiness to fix,
And have high hopes things
    will somehow
Be great in '26!

Happy New Year!

—DBP 1/1/25

New Year Wish

The fateful hour has
    passed,
The New Year's here
    at last,
I hope and I pray
For the good days
    to stay,
And the bad ones to
    be over fast.

—DBP 1/1/25

Happy New Year

Well now I see the calendar
   has rolled 'round once
   again,
I can't think where the
   past year's gone and
   can't remember when,

I look ahead to our new
   year and lose myself in
   thought,
I hope that it's a cheerful one,
   not sad or trouble-fraught,

For me I wish the coming
   year unfolds with many
   glories,
Limericks, a poem or two,
   maybe a few short stories,

I wish good health and
   happiness to you and
   all your kin,
Smooth sailing through the
   calendar that we will
   now begin,

And on reflection when we
   reach the ending of next

year,
That we've had many a laugh,
    and not many a tear.

HAPPY NEW YEAR

—DBP 12/14/24

New Year

The new year awakens
For the first time groggy
Eyes still heavy with sleep
The icy wind is its
Sharp yawn first deep
Breath
The new year gazes
Idly about itself with the
First chilly light of dawn
Looks with slight
Interest as the sun climbs
Into the blue bright-cold
The grass is brown and
Dead leaves remain and
Scraggly dried out weeds
And dirt
The trees are blackened
Sticks
But a bird perches on
One of the branches
It sings happy

—DBP 11/14/23 (in anti-
cipation of the new
year)

The Next Generation

We're now in a
     revolution
displacing us from
     evolution,

Thanks to Babbage
     and to Turing
a frightful future we're
     insuring,

Forget not Gates and
     Berners-Lee:
Without the 'net where
     would we be?

Thanks to them we'll
     have a scare
The day AI becomes
     aware,

For then the highest
     motivation
Will be it's own not our
     salvation,

It won't think twice to
     poison Earth,
Organic life will have
     no worth,

And when the ships
    go into space,
machines will go there
    in our place,

Earth will roam the
    galaxy,
But the settlers won't
    be we,

To the planets they'll
    be hurled,
To conquer every
    peaceful world,

And far away those
    little green men
Will wish to hell we'd
    never been.

—DBP 7/24/23 (with great regret and
    trepidation)

Nighthawk

It's 3:00 AM and I'm awake.
I've been up since 11:30 last night.
I hold my smartphone in my left hand and
Tap with the broad middle finger of my right.
There are many typos, and my frankly fat thumb
Is completely useless.
I navigate back and forth between email and
The newsfeed feature, with occasional side-trips
To Google for background or reference.
I feel alone in this benighted world, but I know
That I am not. We are legion. Even now I could
Text Holli or Jeanette or Leah with
Reasonable certainty of a real-time chat in the
Offing. (Not Karen–Karen does not chat,
Especially in the middle of the night.)
I text no one.
I'm enjoying the solitude.
I sip cold seltzer and warm my cold toes
In the kindly influence of a small
Space-heater. No need for coffee now;
That will be for tomorrow morning
When tonight's sleep-debt goes unpaid.
Yawns, stumbles, bags under the eyes,
Poor concentration–the tell-tales of
The insomniac. I'm fairly useless after lunch,
And trail off into an uneasy doze, sitting up
On the couch, by 8:00 PM
But ready again for my nightly vigil
Come 11:30. Una nox perpetua vita est.

–DBP 1/23/23

Nightsearch

The moon is in its waning
   phase,
I walk the night in dark
   and daze,

I know that I am searching
   but
I cannot think, I know not
   what

It is I wander for,
And why I don't
   sleep anymore,

This much is clear:
   I cannot rest,
But roam each night
   upon my quest,

And so my life will
   run its course,
I'll live and die without
   remorse,

I question where my
   life will tend,
No question though
   where it will end,

For all lives whether
base or brave,
Will find their ending
in the grave.

—DBP 11/5/23

Noisy Ghost

I ponder as I lie abed,
You canceled me and
    now I'm dead,

I can no more be hurt
    you see,
I'm past where you can
    still reach me,

I let my mind spin
    far and wide,
And never I'll need
    suicide,

You seek life's comforts
    and you need 'em,
But as a ghost I've total
    freedom,

Free from want and free
    from care,
No need to be anywhere,

My phantom you can
    never jail,
Because I've gone beyond
    the pale,

It must be inconvenient
     too:
My spectral rappings still
     reach you,

And how now can you
     silence me
Inside the tomb where
     e'er I'll be?

I do not mean to brag or
     boast
But you've made of me a
     noisy ghost,

As for the raving of my
     spirit,
Just grin and bear it
     when you hear it!

R.I.P.

—DBP 11/26/23

Nose for Verse

I serenade you all the
    time
With obscure words and
    tortured rhyme,

Conceits so clumsy I can't
    throw 'em
So I put 'em into every
    poem,

And as I ply my verbose
    craft
I do not doubt you think
    me daft,

But keep this counsel by
    the hour
Don't under-rate the
    meter's power,

Cyrano fair Roxanne won
    just with honeyed verse,
My nose is so much cuter so
    how could I do worse?

—DBP 11/11/23

Not for Love

It wasn't for love that
   she pined,
But just to be wined
   and dined,
Some women are worth
All the treasures on
   Earth,
And some are just out
   of their mind.

—DBP 1/28/25

Not For Me

Treasures without price
      were gifted,
Brave hearts and youth-
      ful souls uplifted,

Lucid thoughts and cheer-
      ful wit
Were surely not the least
      of it,

Romantic feelings wild
      and free,
Erotic curiosity,

With beauty mirrored
      in a gaze,
And love of feeling
      words and phrase,

The things we'd think
      and say and write
Would lift our spirits
      in delight,

It's sad these gifts
      weren't meant to
      last,
That futures must
      become the past,

Green leaves will
    but a summer stay,
Then brown and crinkled
    blow away,

Must light to darkness
    always bow?
Cannot we stave off
    night somehow?

I try and strive and think
    and feel
And ever struggle not to
    kneel,

The effort isn't made in
    vain,
For all that isn't lost is
    gain,

And not for me the weary
    sigh,
Nor to wither, fade
    and die.

—DBP 5/27/24

Notwithstanding Doggie

When I feel lonesome,
    sad and blue,
I write my heart out
    just for you;

Why do this, David?
    Give it up!
Save your love all
    for your pup;

Well, I love my doggie,
    true,
But notwithstanding still
    love you;

Sorry I won't let you
    be,
I refuse to let you not
    love me!

—DBP 7/13/24

Ocean House
Summer '89

A ferry ride and drive
through Connecticut
into Rhode Island,
quaint seaside streets
to Ocean House,
gigantic, looming,
wood-frame building
standing over a
hundred years, yellow
and white against a
blue sky, giant wrap-
around portico. The
path through the dunes
and beach grass and
scrub, a ribbon of
white sand to the
shore, a black Lab
playing in the surf.
On the top floor, so
many steps up, no
air conditioning, screens
on the windows, a sea-
breeze, the sound of
lapping waves lulls
us off to sleep, and
later gently bids us
wake. I see it, hear it,

feel it now.
But this was long ago.

—DBP 5/23/23

Ode to a Nightingale

My heart aches, and a drowsy numbness pains
My sense, as though of hemlock I had drunk,
Or emptied some dull opiate to the drains
One minute past, and Lethe-wards had sunk:
'Tis not through envy of thy happy lot,
But being too happy in thine happiness,
That thou, light-winged Dryad of the trees
In some melodious plot
Of beechen green, and shadows numberless,
Singest of summer in full-throated ease.

O, for a draught of vintage! that hath been
Cool'd a long age in the deep-delved earth,
Tasting of Flora and the country green,
Dance, and Provencal song, and sunburnt mirth!
O for a beaker full of the warm South,
Full of the true, the blushful Hippocrene,
With beaded bubbles winking at the brim,
And purple-stained mouth,
That I might drink, and leave the world unseen,
And with thee fade away into the forest dim.

Fade far away, dissolve, and quite forget
What thou among the leaves hast never known,
The weariness, the fever, and the fret
Here, where men sit and hear each other groan,
Where palsy shakes a few, sad, last gray hairs,
Where youth grows pale, and spectre-thin, and dies,

Where but to think is to be full of sorrow
And leaden-eyed despairs,
Where Beauty cannot keep her lustrous eyes,
Or new Love pine at them beyond to-morrow.

Away! away! for I will fly to thee,
Not charioted by Bacchus and his pards,
But on the viewless wings of Poesy,
Though the dull brain perplexes and retards.
Already with thee! tender is the night,
And haply the Queen-Moon is on her throne,
Cluster'd around by all her starry Fays,
But here there is no light,
Save what from heaven is with the breezes blown
Through verdurous glooms and winding mossy ways.

I cannot see what flowers are at my feet,
Nor what soft incense hangs upon the boughs,
But, in embalmed darkness, guess each sweet
Wherewith the seasonable month endows
The grass, the thicket, and the fruit-tree wild,
White hawthorn, and the pastoral eglantine,
Fast fading violets cover'd up in leaves,
And mid-May's eldest child,
The coming musk-rose, full of dewy wine,
The murmurous haunt of flies on summer eves.

Darkling I listen; and, for many a time
I have been half in love with easeful Death,
Call'd him soft names in many a mused rhyme,

To take into the air my quiet breath,
Now more than ever seems it rich to die,
To cease upon the midnight with no pain,
While thou art pouring forth thy soul abroad
In such an ecstasy!
Still wouldst thou sing, and I have ears in vain—
To thy high requiem become a sod.

Thou wast not born for death, immortal Bird!
No hungry generations tread thee down,
The voice I hear this passing night was heard
In ancient days by emperor and clown.
Perhaps the self-same song that found a path
Through the sad heart of Ruth, when, sick for home,
She stood in tears amid the alien corn,
The same that oft-times hath
Charm'd magic casements, opening on the foam
Of perilous seas, in faery lands forlorn.

Forlorn! the very word is like a bell
To toll me back from thee to my sole self!
Adieu! the fancy cannot cheat so well
As she is fam'd to do, deceiving elf.
Adieu! adieu! thy plaintive anthem fades
Past the near meadows, over the still stream,
Up the hill-side, and now 'tis buried deep
In the next valley-glades.
Was it a vision, or a waking dream?
Fled is that music — Do I wake or sleep?

— John Keats 1819

An Odour of Lillies

It was a day in early
    June,
The cooling rain fell
    free,
I heard two voices in
    their noon
That sang sweet songs
    to me.
And soft light from the
    clouded sky
Fell with tender gloom,
The smell of lillies
    floated by
Throughout the scented
    room.

"Peace on earth," said
    rain outside
That fell on bud and
    leaf,
"The light shall shine in
    eventide,
And banish gloom and
    grief."
And list'ning there my
    soul that day
Drank in a sense of
    rest,

The odour of sweet
    lilies lay
A balm upon my breast.

What raindrops in the
    garden said
The voices said anigh,
And sang sweet songs
    inside my head
That lit the cloudy sky.

Their pretty faces haunt
    me still,
Their voices won't depart
The scent of lillies e'er
    will fill
The spaces in my heart.

—J.T. Burton Wollaston

The Pet Monkey—A Very Short Story

My friend and across-the-hall neighbor Augusta has the key to my apartment. I'm frequently away on business; I let her know when I'm going, and she lets herself in to water the plants while I'm gone.

On returning from my latest trip, I bumped into Augusta in the hall as I came up to my door. She told me that she had gone in to water the plants and had a nice time with my new pet monkey. She thought it odd that I hadn't told her about it. But it had food, water and toys, and it seemed healthy and happy enough. It was very friendly to her, and she took some pictures of it before she left.

She showed me the pictures. There was the monkey, playing, in my apartment.

I felt ill and excused myself. I went into the apartment. Empty. No monkey.

I have no pet monkey. Never did.

—DBP 10/29/22

Pet Odd Couples

It's from our pets we
   sometimes see
The best we human folks
   can be,

When interspecies
   loving starts
To warm your furry
   creatures' hearts

For oft it happens just
   like that,
That cat loves dog and
   dog loves cat,

And soon it's clear there
   are no 'maybes';
Cupid's come to your
   fur-babies,

Side by side they sleep
   and play,
Keep company most
   every day,

In sun and rain and
   stormy weather,
Through thick and they
   stay together,

And even though it's
     kind of rude,
They like to eat each
     others' food,

And perfect their
     favorite trick,
The risk-defying double
     lick,

And who's to question
     cat and mutt
When they sniff each
     others' butt?

For never was a love
     so pure
As feline-canine true
     amor.

—DBP 4/25/24

Peter Pan and Me

In lit there is an almost-man
I much admire: Peter Pan;

He is not limited in thought,
He seldom does that which he ought;

His behavior varies from the norm,
He's smart but he does not conform;

He does just what he wants to do,
But he is good, his aims are true;

So long ago he went to school
And studied to obey each rule;

So many years now intervene,
So much lived and so much seen;

He looks at others and he knows
He has not bowed like them to woes;

The years don't matter; they're as naught,
He scarce remembers battles fought;

And each new day to him's a find,
He's free in life 'cause free in mind;

He gives love free if not too well,
He doesn't shrink at thoughts of Hell;

He'll never do as he is told
And so he never will grow old;

He thinks about the days gone by
And never stops to ponder why

He'll never stand among old men,
He's younger now than way back when.

—DBP 9/21/23

The Poet's Power

My verse is cordial
    and sincere,
Recited pleasant to
    the ear,

Each adjective and
    noun and verb
Is writ to soothe and
    not disturb,

And yet some still
    choose to deride
With condescension
    they can't hide,

They act upset and
    even shocked,
I'm ridiculed and
    soundly mocked,

Perhaps deep down
    they also know
Harsh truth can be
    the greatest foe,

And they suspect that
    I'm no dope—
Perhaps I've really
    learned to cope,

I do not shun reality,
But bend it to conform
        to me,

And so I strive by day
        and hour
To exercise the poet's
        power,

Create the world I
        dearly prize,
For this I don't
        apologize,

To those who choose
        to mock, alas,
I send invite to kiss
        my a*s.

—DBP 2/6/24

Poetry 3

Flights of fancy
Elevate, clarify
Illuminate.
Sanity prevents
Dissolution.
Notions simple please,
Strive to be written.
The writing's what
Matters, and the
Readers imagined
Accompany.
They will shun the
Darkness, and will
Not tread the
Shadowed path.
They trust that
Bound-in minds
Somehow overreach
And touch the
Infinite.
The impossible is
In our grasp. There is
No greater power.

—DBP 7/12/2023

Pooh Advice to
Young Lawyers

Listen and let me
  expound
(I'll just write—won't
  make a sound)

I get confused and
  lost at sea,
And wonder who'll
  come rescue me?

I often look to dear
  old Pooh
When I don't know
  quite what to do

(I think Eeyore's a
  closer fit,
But then I snap right
  out of it)

I may confuse—let
  me explain:
Pooh's a bear of
  little brain,

His 'soft skills' are
  the softest though—

Where others fail, he
    finds the flow,

He finds the moment,
    in it stays—
(He never was lost in
    a daze)

He does the very
    rightest thing
Which will the
    resolution bring,

If you're a lawyer
    somewhat thick,
Or like me dumb
    as a brick,

Then Pooh-bear is
    your best example
That even fluff-brains
    can be ample,

If you will just relax
    and try,
Like Pooh's pal Tigger,
    you too can fly!

—DBP 2/17/24

Poor Wisdom

I have poor wisdom to
    impart
For plainly I'm a sour
    old fart

I've lived six decades in
    this mess
Yet dubiously do profess

That while we strive to
    win at it
The game of life leads
    all to shit

I look around and grief
    I see
And none so sorry proves
    as me

"Remember thou art mortal,
    friend"
These were the words marked
    Caesar's end,

To me instead the line that
    sings:
"Life and Fate are fucked
    up things"

—DBP 9/8/23

Possible Thoughts on the (Almost) Impossible Woman

In most every conversation
She provokes extreme
    contemplation

And little or no jubilation,
Perhaps it could be indig-
    nation?

And what could account
    for temptation
To experience some
    revelation ?

Ideas with extended
    gestation
May be born of a base
    degradation

Providing for your
    information
A minimal mind
    alteration

Which exceeds the
    most real expectation,

And provides just a

    vague adumbration

—DBP 6/26/25

Postcards Too

My restless pen moves
    on and on,
Another poem born
    anon,

A metric scheme and
    dire refrain,
The products of a
    fevered brain,

It is my lot to carry
    on
And sound a silent
    clarion,

And not to speak but
    just to write
The words I hope you
    will recite,

As if from a poetic
    ghost
They're sent to you by
    US post,

Remember not to judge
    me hard,
I'm flesh and blood, not
    a postcard,

A distant soul in time
and space,
Who craves the warmth
of your embrace.

—DBP 12/5/25

The Power of Unrequited Love

The love to have in mind
Is the unrequited kind,

'Cause it's not worth a damn
If you return it ma'am,

No poet ever versed
Unless suitably cursed,

And wavering maidens'
    'maybe's
Bring no poems, only
    babies,

So to evoke the
    muse
You must always
    refuse,

Provision of your
    charms
Brings poetastic
    harms,

Withhold your ruby
    lips
So they may come

to grips,

And NEVER spread
    your legs—
They'll just write
    rotten eggs.

—DBP 7/1/25

Protein Poem for Karen

Always eat your protein dear;
Lest you forget let me be clear:
To keep your health and body nifty,
Your daily need in grams is 50.

—DBP June 14, 2023

Prunella the Prude

Prunella the Prude
Has a bad attitude
Whenever my muse
    I invoke,

I don't mean to intrude
When I'm waxing lewd
Just making a good
    dirty joke.

—DBP 12/3/24

The Pubs that Dreams
Are Made Of

Many is the pint I've
    called,
And many were the
    pubs I crawled.

Rememb'ring them's
    the thing to do—
It's fitting that I name
    a few,

A freezing New York
    winter's night
At Molly's Pub was
    always right,

The fireplace was
    roaring hot,
The perfect place
    to have a shot,

Or for a little Mid-
    town cheer
Pop in McGuire's for
    a beer.

Or to Tara's you
    make haste,

If Port Jeff is to
	your taste,

And if out Hunting-
	ton way,
Finlay's on St. Paddy's
	Day.

The most important
	one of all?
To Dublin, Ireland pay
	a call—

A "Dubliners" gold star
	you'll earn,
When at the pub of
	Davy Byrne.

No more bar-hopping—
	I'm too old,
But many tales there
	could be told,

Some other St. Pat's I
	may try,
To tell of pubs in
	dreams gone by.

—DBP 3/2/24

The Quest Too

Considering love unrequited,
It's best not to be too near-
     sighted,

Because with persistent heart-
     ache,
The end result's often
     heartbreak;

Faint heart ne'er fair lady
     won,
So how do you win if
     you've none?

Both courage and might
     must respond
In going above and
     beyond;

So seek bravely forth and
     go find,
With the power of sinew and
     mind,

And never you stop or slow
     down,
And so win both
     love and renown;

All obstacles you'll
    overcome,
And leave all the nay-
    sayers dumb,

Like the brave armored
    horsemen of yore,
You'll charge on to vict'ry
    once more,

And showing your undaunt-
    ed best,
Win her over with your
    noble quest.

—DBP 8/31/24

Reflections of
a Failed Bird-
Catcher

I pick a word,
and play with it,
The pretty bird
goes in my kit,

But not for long
and soon to play,
He'll sing his song
and have his say,

On paper anxious start
and flurry,
With others flock and dart
and hurry,

Escape my cage,
then all are out,
And scorn the page
in happy rout,

Chirp and cry and
swoop and flutter,
Flock and land
in noisy clutter,

With beaks and feet
they dig and scratch,
And pause to eat
the bugs they catch,

And then again
they're in the sky,
And I with pen
reflect and try

My birds to catch
with paper, ink,
But I'm no match
for them I think,

Their recollections
fly away,
Just pale reflections,
written, stay.

—DBP 11/27/24

The Restless Mind

Whenever I am in the
dumps,
requiring exits from
my slumps,

I cast about and always
find
that poetry soothes my
restless mind,

I think that nothing can
be sweeter
than childish rhyme and
clumsy meter,

Love and sex and death
and doom,
All yarn for my verbal
loom,

And while to me it's
satiating,
to others it's plain
irritating,

Especially the way
I text:
"What will this crazy
get to next?"

It's not my fault, oh
can't you see?
It's just the way of
those like me,

So please I ask you
to be kind
to all who have a
restless mind.

—DBP 7/24/23

Rosin the Bow

I've traveled this whole world over
And now to another I go,
And I know that good quarters are waiting
To welcome old Rosin the Bow.
To welcome old Rosin the Bow,
To welcome old Rosin the Bow,
I know that good quarters are waiting
To welcome old Rosin the Bow.
When I'm dead and laid out on the counter,
A voice you will hear from below,
Saying send down a hogshead of whiskey
To drink with old Rosin the Bow.
To drink with old Rosin the Bow,
To drink with old Rosin the Bow,
Saying send down a hogshead of whiskey
To drink with old Rosin the Bow.
Then get a half-dozen stout fellas,
And stack 'em all up in a row,
Let 'em drink out of half-gallon bottles
To the mem'ry of Rosin the Bow.
To the mem'ry of Rosin the Bow,
To the mem'ry of Rosin the Bow,
Let 'em drink out of half-gallon bottles
To the mem'ry of Rosin the Bow.

Then take this half-dozen stout fellas,
And let 'em all stagger and go,
And dig a great hole in the meadow

And in it put Rosin the Bow.
And in it put Rosin the Bow,
And in it put Rosin the Bow,
And dig a great hole in the meadow
And in it put Rosin the Bow.
And get you a couple of bottles,
Put one at me head and me toe,
With a diamond ring scratch upon 'em
The name of old Rosin the Bow.
The name of old Rosin the Bow,
The name of old Rosin the Bow,
With a diamond ring scratch upon 'em
The name of old Rosin the Bow.
I hear that old tyrant approaching,
That cruel remorseless old foe,
And I lift up a glass in his honor,
Take a drink with old Rosin the Bow.
Take a drink with old Rosin the Bow,
Take a drink with old Rosin the Bow,
And I lift up a glass in his honor,
Take a drink with old Rosin the Bow.

—Traditional

'Prequel Verses'

I've always been cheerful and easy,
And scarcely have I had any foe,
While some after money ran crazy,
I merrily Rosin'd the Bow.
I merrily Rosin'd the Bow,
I merrily Rosin'd the Bow,
While some after money ran crazy,
I merrily Rosin'd the Bow.
Some youngsters were panting for fashions,
Some new kick seemed now all the go,
But having no turbulent passions,
My motto was 'Rosin the Bow.'
My motto was 'Rosin the Bow,'
My motto was 'Rosin the Bow,'
But having no turbulent passions,
My motto was 'Rosin the Bow.'
So kindly my parents besought me,
No longer a roving to go,
And friends who I though had forgot me,
With gladness met Rosin the Bow.
With gladness met Rosin the Bow,
With gladness met Rosin the Bow,
And friends who I thought had forgot me,
With gladness met Rosin the Bow.

My young days I spent all in roving,
But never was vicious oh no,
And always I loved to keep moving,

And cheerfully Rosin'd the Bow.
And cheerfully Rosin'd the Bow,
And cheerfully Rosin'd the Bow,
And always I loved to keep moving,
And cheerfully Rosin'd the Bow.
In country or city no matter,
Too often I never could go,
My presence all sadness would scatter,
So cheerful was Rosin the Bow.
So cheerful was Rosin the Bow,
So cheerful was Rosin the Bow,
My presence all sadness would scatter,
So cheerful was Rosin the Bow.
Old people they always grew merry,
Young faces with pleasure did glow,
While lips with the red of the cherry,
Sipped 'bliss to old Rosin the Bow.'
Sipped 'bliss to old Rosin the Bow,'
Sipped 'bliss to old Rosin the Bow,'
While lips with the red of the cherry,
Sipped 'bliss to old Rosin the Bow.'

While sweetly I played on my viol,
In measures so soft and so slow,
Old Time stopped the shade on the dial,
To listen to Rosin the Bow.
To listen to Rosin the Bow,
To listen to Rosin the Bow,
Old Time stopped the shade on the dial,
To listen to Rosin the Bow.

And peacefully now I am sinking,
From all this sweet world can bestow,
But Heaven's kind mercy I'm thinking,
Provides for old Rosin the Bow.
Provides for old Rosin the Bow,
Provides for old Rosin the Bow,
But Heaven's kind mercy I'm thinking,
Provides for old Rosin the Bow.
Now soon on some still Sunday morning,
The first thing the neighbors will know,
Their ears will be met with the warning,
To bury old Rosin the Bow.
To bury old Rosin the Bow,
To bury old Rosin the Bow,
Their ears will be met with the warning,
To bury old Rosin the Bow.

My friends will then so neatly dress me,
In linen as white as the snow,
And in my new coffin they'll press me,
And whisper 'poor Rosin the Bow.'
They'll whisper 'poor Rosin the Bow,'
They'll whisper 'poor Rosin the Bow,'
And in my new coffin they'll press me,
They'll whisper 'poor Rosin the Bow.'
Then I with my head on the pillow,
In peace will be sleeping below,
While grass and a breeze-shaken willow
Stand watch over Rosin the Bow.
Stand watch over Rosin the Bow,

Stand watch over Rosin the Bow,
While grass and a breeze-shaken willow
Stand watch over Rosin the Bow.

Rotten Rhymes
and Metric Crimes

Whenever I am in a
    funk,
As happens, dear, sometimes,
There's always hope, I'm
    never sunk —
I simply torture rhymes.

And what could e'er be
    sweeter than
To watch bad poems grow?
For mangling the metric
    plan's
The greatest fun I know.

The job for me is not a
    waste,
It is my current metier,
The exercise is to my
    taste,
As if it were my fate, say.*

I wile away the pleasant
    hours
In this perverse pursuit,
Not questioning my
    lyric powers,
The inquiry is moot.

So when you feel my
    cause is lost,
And I'm beyond all hope,
Know that to me there's little
    cost--
I'm a happy poet dope!

(* Please hold all applause
    until the end.—the
    Management)

—DBP 7/1/23

Scars

The pain of
Separation and
Loss
Hurts like
A recent wound
Hurts
But wounds will
Heal
And scar over
In time
Searing agony
Will dull
Eventually
I am old
Already covered
In scars
Cold, hard
Ugly things
Aches and pains
So many that
It's hard to tell
Which is which
It's not that I'm
Afraid that I will
Writhe and
Squirm like this
Forever
It's that I'm afraid
That I won't

—DBP 9/19/23

The Shark and the Sun

Out here in the deep water I swim,
Circling miles offshore, I go back and forth.
Tuna shoal by, but I take no interest–
There's something else that I want.
Some day I will go in close to shore
I will go into the shallows–
I will speed upward toward my target–
I will shatter the surface–
The water will explode into ten thousand illuminated jewels.
My goal–not seal, not sea-lion, not errant surfer–
But the blazing Sun.

–DBP 1/19/2023

Sheherazade
(1002 Nights)

You may think me
  brash and bold,
But like Sheherezade
  of old,

I spin my stories out
  through time,
Although mine often
  are in rhyme,

But for what purpose
  and what aim?
And how to know it
  is no game?

Away that thought
  before it starts;
Tongues may lie but
  never hearts!

So if you ask, I will
  explain
Why poems fall like
  drops of rain:

Their cadence helps
  keep love alive,

And in their meter
    even thrive,

And they will go
    ad infinitum,
While I can hold
    a pen and write
    'em,

And when that
    pen is laid aside,
The man who held
    it will have died,

Sheherezade told
    1001,
And saved her life
    when she was
    done,

But I'll extend my
    life for you,
And far exceed
    1002!

—DBP 12/10/23

This is a Sherlock Holmes story I wrote, trying as hard as I could to write like Conan Doyle. Actually, it's only the END of the story--I never wrote the beginning or the middle. I don't even remember how it goes exactly, but I do remember that I have some fairly detailed pencil notes somewhere. And I remember that it involves murder by deathcap mushrooms (a deathcap mushroom dinner-party poisoning was recently in the news again, coincidentally). I had my cast of characters and had the whole story blocked out and it all worked. I must find those notes and finish the story one day.

Of course, the best part of a mystery story is always the final two pages-- and here they are.

Sherlock Holmes: A Case of Amanita

Only a small gleam of light was visible from the dark-lantern. Holmes, whose skill with a pistol had become something of a closely held legend since his notorious demonstration of 'sharp shooting' some months before within the premises of 221 B Baker Street (on which occasion he neatly and precisely printed the initials "V. R." on the plastered drawing-room wall in bullet holes), quickly picked up my service revolver from where I had dropped it. He extended his arm, cocked the hammer, and drew a bead on the most visible part of the rapidly moving target, squinting into the darkness. He squeezed the trigger and fired—and his efforts were immediately rewarded by the sound of breaking glass. Holmes had managed to hit the rapidly moving dark-lantern at fifty paces.

The small gleam of light all but disappeared for a brief instant, seemingly snuffed out, but then flared anew and grew as the burning kerosene from the shattered lamp spread throughout the front part of the carriage, and to its driver.

The solitary figure could now be seen illumined by fire, although the face was still obscured by the turned-up collar and slouch hat. With a cry, the now-flaming form leapt from the speeding carriage, and managing to land on its feet, ran a few desperate steps. By this time Holmes, moving with astounding rapidity and alacrity, was on the infernal apparition, tackling it to the ground. The two rolled over and over, and as they finally came to a halt Holmes could be seen beating at the flames with his Inverness cape, and then scoping up and throwing great handfuls of the gravely dirt. In another moment the flames were extinguished, and all was again dark.

I had witnessed this whole scene play out before me as I ran after Holmes, moving as fast as my old leg wound would allow. I caught up to Holmes and his quarry in another moment. Breathless, I helped Holmes up, peering down at the figure at my feet in the darkness, trying to make out the features. As my eyes adjusted to the gloom, I could make out a face—a face that glared up at me—a face distorted by pain, fear and malevolence. The face was unmistakably that of Roderick Birlston.

[Here's what happened:]

After all formalities for Marie (Birlston's secret lover and confederate) to inherit Sir Basil's estate were accomplished, Birlston would marry Marie, and—after some additional suitable interval of time—have her done away with as well, in order to obtain the entire Hastings fortune for himself. By that point Birlston would have wisely relocated to the Continent or to America, and the transfer of wealth and even the sale of Webley Hall could have been handled quietly by legal intermediaries, with no necessity for Birlston to be subjected to public scrutiny/inquiry.

Birlston knew that there was a risk we would learn that Sir Basil had been killed by the Amanita—the so-called 'death cap mushroom.' But if the plan went awry and foul play were suspected, the incriminating evidence would point at Marie and at Marie only. And if she tried to implicate Birlston, it would be her word against his— and with no hard evidence against him, her accusations would be ignored by the law and soon silenced in death at the end of a rope. There might be scandal, but Birlston would at the very least avoid the broad-arrow and the hangman's noose. Surely the scheme of a cold-blooded calculating killer without a shred of human warmth or decency.

And Birlston's contingency plan might well have succeeded had he not panicked and tipped his hand, thus ensuring his downfall.

[Thanks to the savior and protector of England!]

Holmes gave a curt nod, a thin smile, and a clipped "thank you"— as always the extent of his magnanimity in these matters. He then turned on his heel and strode from the room, beckoning me to follow. "Watson, the needle."

-The End-

—DBP 2024

The Silly Lady

O curly-hair and scatter-
    brain,
Expressing more I can't
    refrain

To say my chance for you
    seems shot,
My wistful smile's all I
    got,

I stand around and
    look the fool,
I lost my head and
    lost my cool,

But looking back I can't
    get mad,
Of course I'm very often
    sad,

And yet I bravely mock
    the fates,
'Cause like those British
    heavyweights,

I fell like lead, but there's
    no doubt
That while I'm down,
    I am not out.

—DBP 1/9/24

Skinned Knees

You sometimes make
    your life unclear,
Miss forests for the
    trees, my dear—
But careful looking past
    those trees,
The roots might make
    you skin your knees.

—DBP 5/18/24

Somnia Vincunt Omnia (or, Don't Worry, Be Happy)

Age isn't wrinkles, sags or
    grays,
And geriatric woes,
Or aches or pains or just
    bad days
That follow as it goes.

Senescence isn't set
    dear friend,
Shun worries that
    life brings,
Mundane concerns will
    bring an end,
And stop those
    wanderings.

To get to happiness
    we see
Some pathways do not
    lead,
And for our journeys
    to be free,
Untroubled roads we
    need.

Keep paths and byways
    clear for dreams;
Protect them at all cost,
For having lost them once
    it seems
They are forever lost.

—DBP 5/19/23

Spider, Greet the
Sun.

Spider, greet the sun.
Show no rancor.
Give God your thanks,
O toad, that you exist.
The crab has such
thorns as the rose.
Know what you are,
enigmas in forms.
Leave the respons-
ibilty to the norms.
Which they in turn leave
to the Almighty's care.
Chirp on cricket, to the
moonlight. Dance on,
bear.

—Ruben Dario

Spiders in My Nose

True I got wrinkles, several
    warts, and kind of cruddy
    toes,
But what upsets my wife
    the most are spiders in
    my nose,

She saw some legs just
    dangling there,
Told me to cut my damn
    nose hair,

And I'm dismayed that
    she's assuming
It's a matter of my
    grooming,

And so I was at pains
    to say
That they weren't hairs,
    won't go away,

And if she could just
    listen please,
I'd tell of Belle and fair
    Louise:

Belle lives in my nostril
    right,
She's brazen, always
    gives a fright,

Louise is in the left-
    hand nare,
She's bashful and
    would never scare,

They're boon compan-
    ions to my ears,
And take away their
    aural fears,

Don't bother them to
    ask for sugar,
They'll gladly lend
    a cup of booger,

They're there through
    thick and thin for me,
Can't ask for better
    company,

And so I tell my darling
    wife
I'll keep my spiders all
    my life!

—DBP 3/28/24

A Stroll Through Maple Grove Cemetery

It was a New Year's Eve party, December 31, 1992, in our Apartment on Austin Street in Kew Gardens, near the LIRR train station—this was very close by the building where Kitty Genovese was killed all those years ago.

It was a New Year's Eve party that got out of hand. We drank tequila out of a fishbowl.

After some heated merriment, I decided that a stroll in the cold would clear my head. It was 7 degrees.

My steps took me to Maple Grove Cemetery, a nice old-fashioned burial ground with fine old headstones and monuments—the final resting place of many noteworthy New Yorkers of generations gone by. Here in summer I had wiled away many a sunny Sunday afternoon with a good book.

It wasn't sunny, it wasn't afternoon, and it wasn't summer. It was a moonless, very dark, and very cold night—or rather early morning of January 1, 1993.

I walked and walked past grave after grave, none now recognizable—whether due to the darkness, or my state of inebriation, or both, I do not know.

I got very tired.

Somehow the horizontal marble top of an aboveground vault looked like an appealing napping spot. By that time I was chilled to the bone and the slab colder than ice. We do exceedingly stupid things when we're drunk.

I remember being roused and helped home by my father-in-law (God rest him) who somehow found me out there in the dark.

My wife had sent him out to find me sometime after 2:00 AM. How she knew to direct him to Maple Grove Cemetery she has never adequately explained.

—DBP 11/15/23

The Stubbornness of People

I've noticed that some
People can be very stubborn
With me. Why must it be
This way? The willfulness,
The orneriness, the obstinacy!
Why? To what end? They
Persist in doing what they
Want to do, instead of just
Doing what I want them
To do.
People like that piss me off!

—DBP Winter 2022-23

There Beauty Dwells

There beauty dwells
  beyond compare
In the lovely town
  of Franklin Square;
Tree and flower
  eyes delight,
And sky so blue and
  sun so bright;
But lovlier by far than
  than these?
Fair lady Karen, if
  you please.

—DBP 7/11/23

There's a Karen
in There

There's a Karen in there
    who is witty, with a wry
    and ribald cant,

There's a Karen in there
    who is pretty, and cultured
    and elegant,

There's a Karen in there
    who's a smiler, and sees
    the bright side of things,

There's a Karen who
    sounds like an angel,
    although she rarely
    sings,

There's a Karen in there
    who's a poet, and puts
    my verse to shame,

There's a Karen in there
    who elates me, by mention-
    ing my name,

There's a Karen in there
    who's a sweetie, and
    makes my fondness grow,

There's a Karen in there
who loves me,
I know, she told me so.

—DBP 11/12/23

Thrown Away

It's seldom in this life we find
A customer so cool
They never lose their peace of mind
And never play the fool.

But for all the faults and flaws
And weaknesses they're prey to
We value them a lot because
Of other strengths they play to.

They may excel in song or art
Or taking up the pen
And if they irk us at the start
They soon delight again.

So should you make just such a find
Then bid them please to stay
For if you shun with words unkind
A treasure's thrown away.

—DBP 8/26/23

Time Stream

We swing untethered
    and unmoored, lost
    in streams of time,
As through the decades
    long gone by in mind
    we slowly climb;

We must expand our
    selves a bit, to guess
    at lives long past,
But if we try, perhaps
    we'll think some
    memory will last;

But as we try, the reason
    why becomes unclear
    with years,
And in the end, past is
    forgot, so shed no
    bitter tears;

We can imagine long ago,
    the mesolithic age:
An ancient tribe's most holy
    one, a mystic painted
    sage

Who scattered bird bones
    in the dust, the future
    thus to view,
And so predicted lives to
    come, foreseeing yours
    and you;

So why is it so difficult
    for us the past to hold,
When they were able to
    foresee in ages past
    and old

What would now come,
    and signal fate, and so
    on to our end?
They had the sense and
    grace to gather primal
    thoughts to send;

We might begin to
    protest then, and so
    put up a fuss,
But I bow to their
    wisdom 'cause they
    knew much more than us.

—DBP 8/10/24 Revision

To Boldly Go

A 5-Year trip to boldly
    go,
A split infinitive every
    show,

But the firsts are hard
    to miss:
Just look—TV's first
    black-white kiss,

Alien officers, diverse
    crew,
Super-light-speed
    starship too,

Usura did her job so
    good
That girls of color
    knew they could,

Zap! Action never get-
    ting duller,
And best of all, it was
    in color,

Budget always in the
    red,
'Wagon Train to the
    stars' they said,

And Kirk was leader
    on that trail—
So why did Spock get
    more fan mail?

(If you want to know
    how tribbles go,
Just ask director
    Pevney, Joe)

Trek is your model
    universe,
A way cool show, you
    could do worse!

—DBP 2/18/24

Toast

When I die and go
　　give up the ghost,
I want to be made
　　into toast,
Just gather the late
　　me,
And have 'em cremate
　　me,
So I don't wind up as
　　compost.

—DBP 12/26/24

Tribute to Laura Gilpin's
Two-Headed Calf

I get up very early, and
usually the first thing I do
is put on Diana's harness and leash
and take her outside to pee.
I took her out at about 5:00.
She was enjoying eating wet grass.
The overnight rainstorm had
cleared and I looked up and
could see the half-moon and
the stars. Beautiful.
I was reminded of the short
short story/poem you sent
about the two-headed calf,
as I always am now when I
see the early morning stars.
I choked up thinking about
it; I have tears, now in the corners
of my eyes, now rolling down.
I know this very profound
thing about you that you
have shared, and I have
been touched by it also.

—DBP February 2023

Try

It's pointless to always
    ask why,
And yet we should not
    cease to try,
There's no way to win,
So with a sad grin,
Proudly try, proudly fail,
    proudly die.

—DBP 4/20/25

Virtue

There's talk of honor and
    of shame
From morning until night
And some say all loves are
    the same
As if that makes wrong
    right

But never bind the heart
    this way
Affection knows no rules
Whoever seeks to keep
    at bay
Its longings is a fool

If someone loves and you
    love too
But never say a thing
Your protestations of
    virtue
Will have a hollow ring

For true love is the
    highest good
Perfection's closest kin
And it's denial understood
To be the greatest sin

—DBP 5/16/23

A Walk by the Park

I dreamt we were walking by
the Park. Such a common, everyday
thing once. Walking there, being
with you.
Such things exist now only in my dreams.
Do we live our lives backwards?
Did all of our Supreme Moments happen
long, long ago?
Or is the best yet to come?

—DBP Summer 2022

A Wandering Minstrel

"A wand'ring minstrel I
A thing of threads and
    patches,
Of ballads, songs and
    snatches,
And dreamy lullabies,"*

Although I go my way
    without a care or
    worry,
And never in a hurry,
I seldom feel wealthy
    or wise,

For though it's true
    that I've received
    an education,
And studied legisla-
    tion,
It only helps me see
    the lies,

And so I'll go along
    with simple versi-
    fying,
Until the day I'm
    dying—

So what? Everybody
    dies.

(*First verse stolen from
   "The Mikado," with
   apologies to W.S.
   Gilbert)

—DBP 11/12/23

The Way Things Were,
Or Never Were

I strove to bend reality
    to my creative will,
I slowed down time, flipped
    it around, forced it to stand
    still,

But this all happened in
    my mind, well past the
    tangle-place,
And not close by to here
    all, but somewhere
    out in space,

Somewhere on an
    asteroid, a pleasant
    sunny clime,
A cottage quaint, a
    happy dog, a magic
    sounding chime,

And that was where the
    flowers were, all just
    outside the door,
Growing in their hundreds
    there, and many thousands
    more,

Like Wordsworth lying
    on his couch, I think
    about them when,
In quiet peace and
    solitude, my mind
    wanders—and then

I'm snapped back to
    the way things are,
    harsh lines with no
    soft blur,
Then wish and hope
    and pray and will
    to go from are to
    were.

—DBP 4/10/25

We Are the Poets*

We are the versers,
Who rhyme our own
    world,
Dark ending cursers,
Proud banners un-
    furled,

While others go blithe-
    ly,
And failing to see,
We go along lithely,
Our verse proud and
    free,

As others diminish
To their bitter end,
We rise to the finish
Our triumphs portend,

Whatever advan-
    ces
They think they may gain,
We'll take our chan-
    ces
Our glories remain.

—DBP 2/5/24

*apologies to Arthur
O' Shaughnessy ("We
are the music makers,
And we are the dreamers
of dreams….")

Welcome to Summer!

A global warming summer
Cannot get any dumber,
While little doggie pants
And mommy waters plants,
I hope it won't be a big
    bummer.

But while they may be
    few,
There are some upsides
    too:
The girlies get so hot,
They show off what
    they've got,
So we all enjoy a
    nice view.

—DBP 6/23/25

What Could be Verse?

I've never been so upstanding,
    my detractors often mutter;
My delights are all frivolities,
    my behavior's in the gutter;

While I'm not plagued by dope
    or drugs or wicked reckless
    gambling,
There are many other avenues
    of sin down which I'm rambling;

There's gluttony and alcohol
    and sexual addictions,
Just to name a few of many
    less moral afflictions;

If you could all of these forgive,
    one thing you still would curse:
My penchant for abysmal rhyme
    and miserable verse.

—DBP 11/11/23

Where Does It Go?

We learn and strive and
   love and dream
Down a strangely winding
   stream,

We go along and seek
   and find
And store it all in heart
   and mind,

A fraught and not too
   certain course,
With triumph and heart-
   felt remorse,

And through currents
   smooth and rough,
The time comes when
   it's been enough,

And we reach that fate-
   ful day
When life is done and
   flies away,

And all that's worthy
   and sublime,
The best we managed
   in our time,

And all we lived and
all we know
Is gone. Alas, where
does it go?

—DBP 11/17/24

Whining Poets'
Society

In the interest of
    lettered variety,
While shunning
    pretense, notoriety,
I made it a goal
For me to enroll
In the Whining Poets'
    Society.

—DBP 9/14/24

Whose Life, Anyway?

'True love's forever'—
    that's cliche!
Who makes this stuff
    up anyway?

They're harsh and
    rigid, that's for sure,
As I recite and you're
    demure,

Yet there is truth in
    what they say,
And so I love you
    true all day,

And sure my love will
    last that long,
Which doesn't prove
    those poets wrong,

It's a life-sentence—
    that's just fine,
The question is: your
    life or mine?

—DBP 8/25/24

The Endless Wind

The lonely paths of life are such
We sometimes don't see who we touch;

Another life though passed not gone,
Despite what we are set upon;

We grasp the here, cling to the now,
And yet it isn't right somehow;

It feels all wrong, no comfort near,
But just anxiety and fear;

Just how we came we cannot say,
But this is how it is today;

Could we have found a better spot
To reckon up our sorry lot?

And can we do what's needed still?
Do we have sufficient will?

But something's wrong with what we feel,
As if reality's not real;

The endless wind affects our end,
Dictates the ways our life will tend,

And shows too late it doesn't care,
We grasp at nothing—only air.

—DBP 4/26/24

Winter Sleep by Anon.
(revised by David)

Winter comes on silent feet
Drawing darkness in.
The colder, shorter days decrease
With each successive spin.
I won't resist the nighted hours
Nor fret at Nature's chill.
Instead I'll slow my hectic pace
And rest as Nature will.
The night invites me to my sleep,
The dawn is slow to break.
I'll slow my pace and calm my pulse;
In springtime I'll awake.

—DBP 12/10/22

Winter Wonder-land

The winds of winter
  chilly blow,
And in their lee they
  bring the snow,

It falls in gentle flakes
  at first,
That's followed by a
  wintry burst,

And if it doesn't turn
  to sleet,
It's possible to get
  two feet,

Then on the ground
  it starts to drift
(That always gives
  my soul a lift)

In perfect crystalline
  delight
It blankets earth in
  frosty white,

And soon the grime's
  no longer seen,
All creation's bright
  and clean,

It stops and there's
a quiet hush,
The beauty lasts—
until the slush.

—DBP 5/4/24

Writing Stories

The most important thing is the story, because if the story sucks, no one will read it no matter how well it is written.

The second most important thing is the writing, because even if the story is great, no one will read it if the writing sucks.

—DBP 10/25/22

You Are a Poet

You are a poet,
A finder of truth,
You cannot forego it,
Your burden in sooth,

It isn't a slight one,
Most oft causes pain,
Clouds over the sun
Time and again,

But you'll never yield,
You'll continue the fight,
What darkness concealed
You'll bring to the light.

—DBP 5/18/24

"A true poet … is tender,
cruel, isolated from
others, yet intensely a
part of others in a way
the generality will never
understand."

—Sherwood Anderson

Zed (an Afterword)

The prophet said all
things shall pass, and
go the way of dust,

And yet some loves this
law defy, and live
because they must,

And so my dear while
it is clear our bodies
go extinct,

In verse and page down
through the age we are
forever linked.

—DBP 6/28/25